THE HEALING POWER OF PEACE AND NONVIOLENCE

Bernard Häring C.Ss.R.

THE HEALING POWER OF PEACE AND NONVIOLENCE

PAULIST PRESS
New York/Mahwah

First published in the United States by
Paulist Press
997 Macarthur Blvd., Mahwah, NJ 07430

Library of Congress Catalog Card No.: 85-63264

ISBN: 0-8091-2800-4

Printed in Great Britain by
Billing & Sons Ltd., Worcester

Contents

Preface

Literature on peace and war has increased enormously in the past few years. In Europe it is number one topic, because people realize that it is nothing less than a question of "to be or not to be".

In the U.S.A. the focus is on nuclear deterrence, and this is understandable. In Europe the strong pacifist movement was initially triggered by the installation of a new generation of nuclear arms, which are said to be necessary for the protection of freedom but would imply, in case of failure, the destruction of entire populations. Yet the most specific fact in this situation is that Christians, Jews and Humanists are turning their attention to the Bible, and especially to the Sermon on the Mount. Catholic, Protestant and Jewish biblical scholars are filling bookshops with scientific and popular writings. David Hollenbach, in his excellent book, *Nuclear Ethics* (Ramsey, N.J., 1983, p. 13), gives witness to this phenomenon drawing attention to various German-language publications.

Why, then, do I add a new book to those already filling the bookshops? I will mention only few of many reasons. I want to open the horizon for the broader, underlying questions. And I want to respond to the appeal of the U.S. Bishops in their pastoral letter, "The Challenge of Peace", with an emphasis that goes far beyond the problem of nuclear armament. So far as I know, no moral theologian or ethicist has given, up to now, systematic attention to a *therapeutic* approach. I have found here and there some remarks, especially among outstanding peace researchers, on the pathological situation. However, none thus far has tried to present a therapeutic spirituality and strategy. This is what I have tried to do in this book, hoping that others will take up the theme and develop it from various points of view.

What encourages me to publish this text is the great attention that my course on the theme found among my students at the Academia Alfonsiana and at the Gregorian University in Rome.

My heartfelt thanks go to Mrs Josephine Ryan who assisted me not only as stylist and typist but also with most valuable suggestions. I also thank Miss Marion McCracken for her revision of the typescript and of various references.

Introduction

Many theological and pastoral concerns flow together into this treatise on the healing power of the gospel of peace and nonviolence.

The fundamental element is a coherent, therapeutic understanding of redemption, reconciliation and liberation, as found in the best Christian tradition. This rules out all the theories on redemption and sacrifice which distort the image of God by an all too human concept of vindictive justice and violence, of reparation and justice which, throughout history, has been so often connected with tendencies to boundless violence by Christians, even in religious conflicts.

The synthesis between the ministry of salvation and healing in the life of Jesus and in the mission entrusted to his disciples will be consistently applied. The good news of peace and nonviolence plays a central role in Jesus' proclamation of salvation, in his healing activity and in his reconciling death.

The very biblical word "peace" (*shalom*, *eirene*) points to the inseparable unity of peace, salvation, wholeness and healing. In this light we draw special attention to the historical experiences of peacemakers, their charisms for making enemies into good friends, their power of healing, especially of healing people's moral and spiritual blindness. One name, St Francis of Assisi, stands for many others.

We shall then see that peacelessness, hatred and especially collective hatred, with its explosions of enmity and violence, are manifestations and causes of grave deviations, anomalies, folly and many other sicknesses.

Today we face the most dangerous collective madness in the threat of annihilation (M.A.D.: mutually assured destruction) by the superpowers and military blocks who, by now, are powerless to free themselves from this madness to which they and all of humanity are hostages. This sickening situation has its imitations in ever-increasing terrorism, aimless killing, kidnapping for ransom, with murder as alternative, the taking of hostages whose only "crime" is their nationality, and so on. Thousands of people are directly or indirectly involved in such barbarous crimes.

Is it not also a sign of widespread anomaly and blindness when even good people believe and firmly assert that the present system of "deterrence" (of M.A.D.) is acceptable or even an obligatory means of assuring liberty and peace? Some call it "a last resort" under certain conditions, yet they tend to justify it even when all those conditions which they say are indispensable for its acceptability are ignored.

Others are so sick and blind that they cite the Second World War as an example of "just war" for the superpower which demanded unconditional surrender and enforced it by dropping bombs on hundreds of thousands of civilians — women, children, old people — in their homes, hospitals, workplaces. Thus they murdered not only countless innocent persons but also the credibility of a great nation which considered itself champion of worldwide liberty and humanity. The millions of otherwise orderly citizens, who celebrated this experience of almost unlimited power, did not even think of the future when other nations would have the same or multiply greater nuclear power.

Today's humanity is suffering an incredible collective neurosis and blindness if they — we! — are unwilling to undertake a heart-searching diagnosis of the growth and perpetuation of this state of "mutual deterrence", with its ever-increasing accumulation of nuclear weapons sufficient to kill all inhabitants of this planet ten times over. And we should include in that search our "faith" in constant expansion of production and consumption: a system whereby the rich become richer and the poor poorer, and a success-oriented education and worldview leads to a ruthless exploitation of the treasures of the earth, to the pollution of water, air, etc., all to the detriment of spiritual health.

The dimensions of the sickness of peacelessness, aggressivity and violence — symbolized in those whose entertainment is to watch cruelty in the movies day by day — becomes even more disturbing if we remember that God in his mercy awoke men like Mahatma Gandhi and Martin Luther King, who have promoted an epoch-making process of healing public life by a spirituality and means of nonviolence, yet the majority of those in responsible positions in our nations dare to ignore this saving road of peace.

Even considerable parts of the increasing peace movements all over the world remain in the narrow circle of protest against nuclear armament instead of giving full attention to the gospel of peace and nonviolent spirituality and action. Many of these good people are still victims of the collective blindness that cannot perceive the healing power of nonviolence. Have we, moral theologians and churchmen, fulfilled our role of healing and revealing in this decisive field?

Only when we are offered and can offer a real alternative and strong remedy will it be possible to search for a clear diagnosis of the destructive sickness of peacelessness and violence and their deeper causes. Many years ago, one of the most competent peace researchers, Carl Friedrich von Weizsäcker, called emphatically for an approach to this problem in the perspective of illness and healing, to no detriment of the ethical dimensions of these problems. He illustrated the situation by quoting Pastor Fritz Bodelschwingh who, by a frank "therapeutic" confrontation with the highest authorities in the Hitler regime, succeeded in saving hundreds of mentally-ill persons entrusted to his institution: "These, my dear friends here, are sick only in their heads, while those in Berlin (those in power) are sick even in their hearts".[1]

The peacelessness that characterizes our epoch has its roots in self-deception and neurosis because of repressed truth. The courage to search for truth and to put into practice that truth, which is healing love, is the very soul of peace and peacefulness.

Weizsäcker's reflections will be the guidelines in this treatise. "Peacelessness", he says, "is not an aspect of human health but of human sickness. It is not something that should exist nor something that unfortunately cannot be changed". He is convinced that peacelessness and violence are an almost inextricable mixture of stupidity and malice; but at the same time he warns against approaching this malady by scolding those who are its captives. "Peacelessness should not be addressed from without either as stupidity or malice; it will not be overcome by indoctrination or by condemnation. Only in the process of healing will the patient become conscious of how stupid he was as a sick man or how guilty as a sinner. The sick, whose illness cannot be healed or is not yet healed, need solicitous care. The healing of peacelessness is, humanly speaking, not possible without a realm of healing which includes solicitude for those not yet healed".[2]

Weizsäcker warns humankind, whose aggressivity got out of control: "In view of his aggressiveness man appears as the sick animal, insane in his innermost being".[3] The sane human being is gifted with speech, with power to communicate within the stream of tradition, able to share with others in the search for saving truth. Those who lack the faculty for truthful communication in the search for peace belong to the most demented species of animal. This becomes clear now, when it is quite evidently a matter of survival of the species, let alone of meaningful personal survival. If humankind, as species, has not the inner strength to accomplish that healing transformation which is indispensable for survival in peace, then there is a clear case of a deadly sickness.

If humankind as a whole is in extreme danger of mutual self-destruction, then there is nothing more important than to join in the wholehearted search for the saving truth and for effective remedies. And there is little chance to find or to offer healing if each of us does not find the courage to face his or her own shades, sickness and blindness. "How can we help the sick if we do not recognize what is sick in ourselves and have not learned to accept the others as sick people?"[4]

The last quote should open our eyes to how seriously a therapeutic approach must be considered in the whole realm of peace and peacelessness. But, as disciples of Christ, it is even more important that we turn our eyes to Christ, the Saviour, the Peace, the Healer, and in his light to discover in ourselves and in others the inner powers for peace and peace-making.

This aspect is concretely expressed by W. Willems:

"Did you ever realize that the nearness of a person can make healthy or sick, can kill or bring to life?

Did you ever realize that the nearness of a person can make good or evil, joyous or sad?

Did you ever realize that a man refusing to come can let die, while his coming can bring back to life?

Did you ever realize that the word and deed of a person can open the eyes and mind of a man who was blind to everything, who had discovered nothing in the world and in his life?

Did you ever realize that the voice of a person can heal a man who was deaf to everything?

Did you ever realize that taking time for your neighbour can mean more than medications, more than money, sometimes even more than a surgery?

Did you realize that listening to people does wonders, that benevolence brings interest, that an advance of trust returns to us a hundredfold?

Did you realize that deeds do more than words?

Did you realize that the road from knowing to doing is far?"

I have purposely chosen the words "*Healing Power*" for the title to make clear from the start that my therapeutic approach has nothing to do with withdrawal or an inactive pacifism. I share with Rollo May the concern not to belittle or deny the need for power or to repress the thought of power. Programmatically, May explains that what he speaks about is "power analogous to the healing power by which one overcomes tuberculosis, not analogous to military power".[5]

It is in this sense that we look for the healing power of nonviolence, without however neglecting the social dimension.

We shall ask ourselves what are the place and role of the gospel of peace and reconciliation and especially of nonviolence in the whole of moral theology and in Christian life (Chapter I).

The situation of today's world can tell us much about the urgency of the gospel of peace and of nonviolent involvement for fostering peace (Chapter II).

We look first to divine revelation and then, in its light, to the signs of the times for the meaning and relevance of nonviolence as expression of redemption and of the divine gift of peace, and as response to the signs of the times (Chapter III).

We study the healing power of nonviolence first, in view of interpersonal relationships, before confronting its crucial problems in fighting against sinful structures and in view of turning enemies into friends (Chapter IV).

While giving priority to the change of heart in the policy of nonviolence in interpersonal relationships, we can turn our attention even more emphatically to its relevance and healing power in all social and political international relationships. We appraise nonviolent revolution and civilian nonviolent defence as healing alternatives to the present armament and nuclear threat, but first in the promotion of healthier and less unjust social-economic conditions. We look for justice and peace everywhere through nonviolent commitment (Chapter V).

We recommend a nonviolent transarmament, with civilian defence as a way to drain away much of the poison from international relationships, and as a healing alternative to the system of deterrence (Chapter VI).

However, we cannot indulge in illusions: we must face the enormous difficulties of transarmament for weapons of peace: spirituality and its practice, and a strategy of civilian defence. But we will also see the unique opportunities for an encompassing healing of public life through all the efforts of preparing for the alternative of nonviolent civilian defence (Chapter VII).

The Church is sent not only to preach the gospel of peace and nonviolence and the effective manifestation of that love of enemies which works for the victory of love and reconciliation; she should also be an effective sign of both in all her life (Chapter VIII).

NOTES

1. C. F. von Weizsäcker, "Friedlosigkeit als seelische Krankheit", in: *Der ungesicherte Frieden*, Göttingen 1979, 32–56, quote 33.
2. *l.c.*, quote 33.
3. *l.c.*, 36. In the same vein, psychotherapist Rollo May, *Power and Innocence. A Search for the Sources of Violence*, New York 1972, writes: "We are the cruellest species on the planet. We kill not out of necessity but out of collegiance to such symbols as the flag and fatherland. We kill on principle". Similarly, Gerard A. Vanderhaar, *Christians and Nonviolence in the Nuclear Age* (Mystic, Conn. 1982), 45: "To build weapons of such destruction and to be ready to use them are marks of a people losing their minds and souls". D. Hollenbach, *Nuclear Ethics*, Ramsey, N.J., 1983, 65: "Deterrence uses irrationality as a tool of political reason". Also, in harsher language, J. Glenn Gray, *The Warriers*, New York 1967, 51: "Human beings can be devilish in a way animals can never be".
4. *l.c.*, 51.
5. R. May, *op. cit.*, 14.

CHAPTER ONE

Foundations of a theology of peace

People who are not deeply shocked by the present armament race and the nuclear "deterrence" programme are gravely sick, inhumane. Apocalyptic pictures from the Book of Revelation (e.g., 8:7–9:2) take on a new, frightening aspect. Those for whom a theology — and particularly a moral theology — on peace and peace mission remains only a marginal question in this historical moment condemn themselves to become altogether marginal.

Every serious politician realizes that peace politics is at the centre now, and that only those policies which consider all the sectors and decisions of politics in the light of peace and peace promotion are worthy of the name "peace politics". It should be, then, even more evident that the evangelization of today's world is possible and sound only if the gospel of peace is made transparent and becomes the yeast in all dimensions of the proclamation of salvation and pastoral care.

1. *Centrality of the promise, gift and mission of peace in revelation*

Many people have discovered anew the centrality of the promise and gift of peace in revelation. The plenary session of the World Council of Churches, 1983, expressed this clearly in its statement on Peace and Justice (n. 9): "The bilblical vision of peace and justice for all, of wholeness, of unity for all of God's people is not one of several options for followers of Christ. It is an imperative of our time". The acceptance of this calling, with the readiness to follow Christ on the road of the cross in fulfilment of our peace mission, is the concrete realization of being church and being Christian.[6]

"Readiness for the gospel of peace" (Eph 6:15) is an all-encompassing programme for every disciple of Christ and for every Christian community. "The gospel does not speak on peace occasionally; peace is not one of the themes among many others, but the central articulation and dynamics; on nothing else does the gospel speak more emphatically and more frequently than on peace".[7] Being at peace with all of God's creation, peace as essential dimension of salvation, the peace of Christ, peace among his disciples, their blessed mission to be peacemakers on earth: all these are dimensions of one and the same mystery.

The biblical concept of peace is amazingly comprehensive. It includes salvation, wholeness, integrity, healthy and healing interpersonal relationships, cultural, economic and social relationships and transformations which serve the cause of peace, of wholeness, of integrity. The Jewish writer Herman Cohen asks: "What is the synthesis and essence of human life in the spirit of the Bible?" And immediately he answers: "Peace! It is the harmony of all energies of life, their balance, and the recognition of all the opposites and conflicts. Peace is the crown of life. Peace makes all of life a feast".[8]

God's reign, promised by the prophets and announced and made visible in Christ, tends to abiding peace. Peace is at the heart of all of God's promises and gifts. It should be expected that this promise and gift should take such hold of the disciples of Christ that they will be ready to dedicate themselves to the gospel of peace. Every Christian, according to his or her capacity, is called to be an evangelist. "It should go without saying that the gospel one represents is the gospel of peace (there being no other gospel). But we will say it anyhow: to become Christian should be identical with being an eschatological peacemaker".[9]

When a Christian is involved in a concrete issue of peace on earth, he should also remain conscious that the gospel is broader, more radiant and more comprehensive than all our endeavours. The activist should honour the witnessing of fellow-Christians to the biblical peace eschatology. Secular activism must never be proffered as a substitute for the Christian's primary witness to the all-encompassing peace of Christ. While emphasizing commitment to peace and justice in the socio-economic field, I agree with Vernard Eller that: "It is not the social activism that makes a peace church a peace *church*".[10]

To be peacemaker and witness to Christ's peace, one has to be deeply touched by faith in God's gift of a peace beyond all human concepts and by the glorious mission for the kingdom of God's peace. Whoever wants to serve this great cause must be guided by the words of a prophet of peace: "Nation shall not lift sword against nation nor ever again be trained for war. O people of Jacob, come, let us walk in the light of the Lord" (Is 2:4–5). That alone is the way "to beat spears into pruning-knives".

The central role of the gift and mission of peace in Revelation has its strengthening counterpart in the signs of the times. "Commitment to peace is not one among many other tasks. It is rather the characterizing task in our world; to fail in this matter would be the most destructive failure".[11] The task is gigantic. It requires a whole new way of thinking and a profound transformation of the socio-economic and political structures to bring about an authentic order of peace and justice.

For this great purpose all people of good will must co-operate. Christians must not and need not ignore their distinctive role. That Christ, the prince of peace and Peace in person, is rule and ruler for our commitment to his gospel of peace belongs to the heart of our faith. Even though some might consider it first as only a way to work for the survival of humankind, the courage and firm option of Christians to dedicate themselves thoroughly to the gospel of peace might well become the best — and perhaps the only — real chance to preach Christ's message and to give witness to it in a way accessible to many people of good will. "What up to now seemed to be disfunctional might well reveal itself as functional; what seemed to be an ethical luxury might well be recognized as the chance for survival".[12] Is today's theology willing and able to see this?

I would like to hope that the earnest invitation of the USA bishops is taken most seriously. "No greater challenge or higher priority can be imagined than the development of a theology of peace suited to a civilization poised on the brink of self-destruction". It is characteristic that these words are part of what the bishops say on nonviolence and the alternative of nonviolent civilian defence, adding that "these principles must be part of any Christian theology of peace".[13]

2. *Peace: A challenge to all of theology*

Useful as particular treatises on peace may be, a theology of peace means much more. All theological endeavours, and particularly efforts to present a synthesis of Christian theology, must make evident the relevance and central role of the gospel of peace. It should become clearer than the sun that this gospel is meant to be and become ever more the yeast of Christian life, individually and socially.

It is especially encouraging that in recent years outstanding biblical scholars, aware of the burning actuality and in dialogue with other disciplines, have dedicated their efforts to the meaning, purpose and horizons of peace, and particularly of nonviolence in the Old and New Testaments.[14] One of the precious results is the clear insight that the point of departure for a theology of peace is not just particular words of Jesus but his whole life, his actions and his death. Due attention is given to the undeniable fact that Jesus understood his mission in the light of the Old Testament theology of the Servant of Yahweh in Deutero-Isaiah. So it is not just a question of an abstract concept of peace but of God acting in Jesus Christ. This becomes most evident in the writings of St Paul and St John, and they shed their light on all biblical texts.

In dogmatic theology there is, for example, a promising sign in the worldwide discussion of the writings of René Girard and in constructive systematic efforts.[15] Girard and theologians who enter into dialogue with his works scrutinize all the theories about sacrifice and the sacrificial death of Christ in order to eliminate whatever suggests a rather violent image of God or injects human violence into God's saving plan.

The words of Raymund Schwager, professor of dogmatic theology, are revealing: "The words of Revelation expose the truth about a sinful world with its lies and aggressiveness, and then gradually show ways of overcoming them. . . . The judging God is not a beating God, but one who accepts being beaten in his own Son. Yet, he does judge men by giving them over to the logic of their own doing. . . . Hence the glory of God is no longer to be looked for in 'holy wars' nor in violent procedures of punishment, but in his Servant and Son who, empowered by the Father, suffers being beaten by evil without beating back and without interiorly succumbing to the evil. It is from this sign of salvation that the call comes to conversion, to liberation from sin, lie and violence".[16]

By giving prime attention to the gospel of peace embodied in Christ and to the Church's mission of peace, dogmatic theology regains its kerygmatic and soteriological dimensions. It also becomes better oriented than in the last centuries to the Church's mission to proclaim salvation and to heal — to be an effective sacrament of peace and reconciliation.

The gospel of peace and the signs of the times constitute the greatest challenge and opportunity for moral theology and missiology. By giving a central role to the gospel and mission of peace and nonviolence, they rid themselves of any possible insinuation of irrelevance in today's peaceless world. They can reach out to a huge, sensitive audience. They regain their prophetic role and healing dynamics in continuity with the mission of the great prophets and especially of Christ, *the* Prophet and Healer: *the* Peace. Through the proper vision of the all-encompassing peace of Christ — peace with the created world entrusted to man, peace of heart and mind, peace among persons and nations — moral theology gains an organic unity and synthesis of individual and social ethics.

The theme of peace should also mark the history of moral theology, its heights and shallow moments, its greater or lesser faithfulness to the revelation of peace, while looking for the causes of a partial alienation and temporary irrelevance.

The dimension of peace is indispensable in treatises on liberty and responsibility, fundamental option, formation of a distinctive Christian conscience, on sin and conversion, on faith and witness to faith, on eschatological hope and people's present hopes and anguishes, on redemptive love and on timely and untimely virtues.[17] It belongs to all parts of social ethics, medical ethics, ecological responsibility, socio-economic life, and particularly to the ethics of politics, the goal of which is a truthful politics of peace, of co-operation for a healthy public opinion, indeed to all facets of human life.

Accepting the challenge of the signs of the times and the contribution of today's biblical studies, a moral theology which gives the gospel of peace its proper place will be better rooted in the Bible and in the dynamics of the history of salvation.

As an example of such renewed biblical approach I might quote Trutz Rendorff on how, in an ethical treatise, he uses exegetical insights. He takes as starting point the words, "Be perfect as your heavenly Father" (Mt 5:48), in its context of God's government in history. "So often we hear that the world cannot be governed by the Sermon on the Mount. A main argument is that there exist enemies. . . . But in God's own perspective we might well be obliged to accept that the world cannot at all be governed without the Sermon on the Mount. For we can live only because we, the world, are judged by God by standards other than those we have deserved. The reason that the world goes on and can succeed is because God is above human behaviour and ingratitude. The world would perish if man's evil, enmity, recklessness in pursuit of self-interest and reaction on the same level would be the measure".[18]

It is not God's way to follow our miserable practices and our tendency towards vindictive justice in the government of the world. Rather, we, the redeemed, should learn from God, who gives rain and sunshine to good and less-good people.

Those who, being justified by faith and undeserved grace (cf. Rom 5:1), have found peace with God should find enough good reasons to follow his example in human relationships. "In other words, the peace of God, which is beyond human understanding (Phil 4:7), does not exclude the sound reasoning of Christians in the world and in their place. Rather, it includes it (cf. the sequence of Phil 4:7 and 4:8). The peace which even reasonable human action cannot provide does, however, set free human intelligence and reason for the concrete questions of how to respond properly to the historic situation".[19] Illumined by the word of God and guided by his own way of acting, a morals of grace meets with a morality of responsibility.

3. *Towards a synthesis between proclaiming peace, promoting peace, and healing*

The synthesis and synchronization of proclaiming salvation and healing the sick in general are imperative for the integrity of the ministry of salvation as well as for the *diakonia* of healing.[20] This is especially urgent for the proclamation of the gospel of peace and the ministry of peace and of healing.

The gospel of peace is not only destined for liberation and justice; it serves also for psychosomatic health, for the sound development of spiritual health, for healthful interpersonal relationships and for healing the socio-economic, cultural and political processes of public life. The more the synergy between ministry of salvation and *diakonia* of healing is understood and put into practice, the more these benefits will accrue. Making this perceptible is one of the main purposes of this treatise.

In this realm, too, the model of the "wounded healer" might be quite helpful for the very purpose of fostering peace and nonviolence as well as for genuinely human health. We have first to seek in ourselves the deepest roots of peacelessness and of temptations to aggressiveness. We will at the same time be able to discover our own inner resources for healing. Then we shall be able to help one another in the double effort of unmasking evil and unhealthy tendencies and of discovering our inner strengths for peace and health. All this will proceed much better if we are strongly motivated by earnest dedication to the gospel of peace. We learn to accept one another, appreciating the good without repressing the recognition of our shadows. Thus we shall join hands in the healing ministry of peace and nonviolence.

"Only the strength of peacefulness fosters peace. Each of us has to heal himself. This, however, does not happen by mere introversion (being busy with oneself) but in the course of a concrete dedication to the cause of peace in the environment which is within our reach. This practical orientation includes, however, the readiness for meditative self-examination".[21] It is part of our tragic situation that those in positions of power or influence are frequently peaceless men or women who refuse to recognize their sickness and their need of healing.

A new way of thinking and of shaping public consciousness would be very helpful. Therefore, Carl Friedrich von Weizsäcker proposes the inclusion of peacefulness and peacelessness into the norm of health versus sickness. "There is good reason to work out a definition of man which implies, of itself, the norm of health that says that man healed from peacelessness is truly healthy. In living together in social life this is the only satisfying and helpful norm. On the other hand, it is eccentric to think that, in an unredeemed world in which peacelessness seems to prevail, we might just leave such a world to itself. By doing so we would deliver it and, at the same time, ourselves to catastrophe".

As committed Christian, the great peace-researcher believes in the power of redemption and in the Christian's mission to proclaim and to foster peace. Hence arises the practical question about a realistic approach. "Loving care for those not yet healed means healing justice and laws, where love has not yet conquered the hearts; canalization of conflicts, wherever we have not succeeded in making them avoidable; and creation of an order of peace, with power humanized as much as possible. It is the same power of peacefulness or — to use another expression — of love of neighbour, which makes healing possible in fortunate cases, and in less fortunate cases allows at least meaningful care".[22]

One of the most deeply rooted causes of the sickness of peacelessness is unbridled aggressiveness. The evil becomes extremely grave when people try to justify their aggressive behaviour on ethical or even religious grounds, while working out all kinds of ideologies. This point deserves special attention.

The pastoral letter of the West German Catholic Bishops, "Justice Creates Peace", points to various forms of injustice as chief causes of increasing conflicts and tensions. The Bishops conclude that therapy for peacelessness proceeds from conversion to justice at all levels and in all interpersonal, social and political relationships. But it is not a question of a one-way relationship. By healing their blindness and turning their hearts towards healing peacefulness, people will begin to understand better what justice requires of them.

The Japanese Hierarchy's pastoral letter on peace denounces the causes of peacelessness, the main ones being practical materialism, striving for superiority, mutual distrust, injustice and tension between the highly industrialized countries and the southern hemisphere. What is needed, above all, is to remove these causes and dismantle "the wall of enmity which separates people".[23]

Reading the major documents on peace and peacelessness issued by the Holy See and by many episcopal conferences, we see clearly that it is not just a matter of imperative morals but, rather, of proclamation of the gospel of peace and of serious search for a diagnosis and effective remedies. The prime remedy is openness to and right understanding of the promise, gift and mission of peace coming from God, with trust in the Holy Spirit who intends to produce in us and through us a harvest of joy, peace, love, gentleness, nonviolence.

Although the perspective of healing is not yet in the foreground of Church documents, it comes more and more clearly into sight. It is an important dimension of peace education, which cannot be rightly understood and implemented without giving earnest attention to the dynamics of therapy.[24] Already the biblical concept of "*shalom*" points in this direction.

4. *Unmasking polluted peace: mission in the strength of truth*

Following the example of the biblical prophets, all shades of liberation theology exercise the ministry of denouncing lying, and foul talk about peace and security, which covers up unjust, sinful and oppressive socio-economic and political structures and activities on the one hand, and lethargy and passive submission on the other. This effort to unmask and awaken is indispensable. Some parts of liberation theology would become more convincing and less frightening if they would give first attention to the therapeutic dimensions of diagnosis and of practical efforts for liberation on both sides. The rich and overprivileged must be freed from their blindness, individual and collective selfishness, superiority complex, refusal to share the power of decision and rewards of common work. The poor must be freed from their fatalism and passivity, freed to discover their own inner resources and the power of solidarity.[25]

The gain or loss of this therapeutic dimension depends on the fundamental option for either nonviolence or for more-or-less ignoring this alternative. Violent revolution is a bloody surgery which, as such, does not contribute to healing. Victorious revolutionaries generally cannot be expected to be well prepared to heal the terrible wounds they have inflicted on their enemies, their own allies and themselves.

If truth is spoken and done in redemptive love, the unmasking of a false peace, with its injustice and deceptions by people who try to cover up peacelessness, is part of a sharing in Christ's peace mission. An essential part of bringing the whole situation into the light of liberating truth is the unmasking of violence in all its forms and with all its ideological "justifications". The powerful who inflict violence on the weak and poor not only try to deceive others; they themselves fall into the fog of their own lies. They are sick. And normally it can be expected that their first reaction against those who try to bring all these things into light will be violence, an expression of their grave disorders.

Jesus, speaking and doing the truth in love, experienced more than anyone else these reactions from the ruling class of Israel, yet he never stopped fulfilling his mission in love. "Father, forgive!".

What matters is that we act in the same way, ready to suffer for the liberating truth of love and the love of truth. The power of truthful peacefulness and the strength of loving truth cause temporary separations and call for firm decisions. Our part can be fulfilled in the footsteps of Christ Crucified, trusting in his grace and in the victorious power of his resurrection which is, above all, the greatest victory of love even in the midst of the greatest conflicts.

NOTES

6. Cf. R. Stahl, "Das Verhältnis von Friede und Gerechtigkeit als theogisches Problem", in *Literaturzeitung* 109 (1984), 162–171.

7. E. Biser, "Gedanken des Friedens", in: F. Henrich (ed.) *Soldat zwischen Verteidigungs- und Friedensauftrag*, Regensburg 1971, 55–74, quote 62.

8. H. Cohen, *Die Religion der Vernunft aus den Quellen des Judentums*, Köln 1959, 531, 523.

9. V. Eller, *War and Peace. From Genesis to Revelation*, Scottsdale 1981, 203.

10. *l.c.*, 204.

11. C. F. von Weizsäcker, *Der ungesicherte Friede*, Göttingen 1979, 108.

12. G. Theissen, *Soziologie der Jesusbewegung*, München 1977, 110f.

13. "The Challenge of Peace: God's Promise and Our Response", text in *Origins* 13 (1983) 21–22.

14. An excellent international bibliography on the latest studies on violence and nonviolence is in: N. Lohfink (ed.), *Gewalt und Gewaltlosigkeit im Alten Testament*, Freiburg in Br. 1983, 225–247. New Testament studies concentrate frequently on the Sermon on the Mount as point of departure. A good bibliography in G. Strecker, *Die Bergpredigt*, Göttingen 191–194.

15. Cf. R. Girard, *La violence et le sacré*, Paris 1972; id., *Des choses cachées depuis la fondation du monde*, Paris 1978; id., *Le bouc émissaire*, Paris 1982. Cf. R. Schwager, *Glaube, der die Welt verwandelt*, Mainz 1976; id., *Brauchen wir einen Sündenbock? Gewalt und Erlösung in den Biblischen Schriften*, München 1978.

16. R. Schwager, in: N. Lohfink, *op. cit.*, 217f.

17. Cf. B. Häring, *Zeitgemässe und unzeitgemässe Tugenden*, Katholische Akademie der Diözese Augsburg 1984.

18. T. Rendtorff, "Grundsätze und Perspektiven zur Friedensethik heute", in: E. Lorenz (ed.), *Kirchen für den Frieden*, Stuttgart 1983, 19–34, quote 33.

19. H. F. Weiss, "Biblische und Theologische Grundlagen für ein Friedensengagement von Christen und Kirche", in: *Kirchen und Frieden*, 35–48, quote 44.

20. cf. B. Häring, *Healing and Revealing. Wounded Healers Sharing in Christ's Mission*, St Paul Publications, Slough 1984.

21. C. F. von Weizsäcker, *op. cit.*, 52.

22. *op. cit.*, 54.

23. Text in: *Stimmen der Weltkirche* (Nr 19): Bischöfe zum Frieden, Bonn 1983, 225–235.

24. Cf. B. Häring, *Umrustüng zum Frieden*, Freiburg 1983; Italian version: *Nuove armi per la pace*, Roma 1984; id., *Free and Faithful in Christ*, vol. 3, St Paul Publications, Slough 1981, 391–426.

25. Cf. *Concilium* 20 (1984), special number on liberation theology. On the crucial point of nonviolence see the document of the Congregation for the Faith of August 6, 1984, XI/7 (pointing also to the document of Puebla II, II, 5, 4).

CHAPTER TWO

Peace, salvation, wholeness and healing in the history of salvation

Only with our eyes on the whole history of salvation can we experience the urgency and density of the present time of salvation. "Today, if you hear his voice, do not grow stubborn as in those days of rebellion". The Letter to the Hebrews (3:7–19) interprets anew these words of Psalm 95 in view of the urgent need for clear decisions in the situation of that community at that moment.

The present situation of the human race is apocalyptic. For the first time in history man is able to bring this very history to a terrible end. This obliges us to see our "today", on one hand, in the light of a long and horrifying history of human aggression, violence, terrorism and vindictiveness, but, on the other, in the light of redemption, the history of salvation, of promise and gift of peace: God himself acting in Christ for peace and human peacefulness.

Exegesis of the New Testament has shown abundantly that the various biblical writers actualize the gospel of peace for their immediate community and historical moment, which they address without detriment to the identity and authenticity of this divine revelation. Therefore, in our decisive "today" we feel the special need" to spell out, in view of the new hearers, the message of God's acting in Jesus Christ to bring forth peace".[26]

1. *Abiding and changing elements in the gift and task of peace*

In all reflections on peace, the point of departure is to be God's own plan and initiative, his thoughts and deeds of peace since the foundation of the world, his creation of man to his image and likeness, in view of the coming of the one who "is our peace" (Eph 2:14), and his promises of final peace. On the other side we see all the aberrations of humankind in violence and war, and the frightening effort to justify them by lies and even by speaking of "holy wars", with destruction and terrible cruelties. It is solely God's faithfulness to himself and his plan that gives us courage and trust in fulfilling our peace-mission despite all the obstacles.

René Girard, professor of comparative culture and literature, has dedicated his research to the causes and consequences of violence since the beginning of human history.[27] He tries to decipher the shocking history of human violence in the light of ethnology, anthropology, ethology and comparative religion. But the dynamics of his reflections show a deep faith that "since the foundation of the world" God, in his plan of salvation, offers redemption and liberation from violence through his Son and Servant, Jesus Christ.

God's plan, fully manifest in Christ, is still hidden to many people, even to many Christians. The present crisis, however, might well be the great chance to understand better God's saving plan, a challenge to humankind — and especially to Christians — to rid itself of violence, deception, oppression, vindictiveness, through that strength of love and truth that can transform enemies into friends.

Girard explains that at the beginning of hominization, marked by an enormous increase in the size of the cerebral cortex, there is also an increasing trend towards mimesis (mimicry). This fosters the capacity to learn, but it also manifests itself in mimicking acts of appropriation and forms of aggression which lead to fighting and even to mutual killing. This is a regression in comparison with earlier forms of animal life where there is little such inclination within the same species.

This new explosion of mimesis — of appropriation and violence — would have led to the extinction of the new species without the development of prohibitions, taboos and discouraging rituals. At the height of the mimetic crisis there came to be — as we can still learn from myths and rituals — the so-called "foundation murder", a sacrificial action of violent character which becomes sacralized. This act is experienced as life-saving, but also as a limit which may not be transgressed. The "victim" is considered as "guilty" and, at the same time, as saving, as dying for others. "At the end of the sacrificial action, this appears to religious societies as conclusion of the crisis, which then continues to be enacted ritually".[28]

For conflict-solving, a ritual synergy between prohibitions and ritual memorial arises. The memorial of the foundational sacrifice gives sanction to the prohibitions. But a memorial of a sacralized act of violence, while it can temporarily set limits to aggressive mimesis, cannot really win freedom from the tendency to violence, since the heart of the matter is "sacralized, justified violence". Therefore, "the crisis must be ritually enacted again and again in order to produce the decision for peace and order".[29]

The prohibitions indicate directly the purpose. They discourage everything that leads to crisis, condemning severely and in the name of the sacred every gesture and kind of behaviour that led to the socially dangerous situation. The enforcing ritual is indispensable. In order to make it tangible and socially effective it indicates that, under similar circumstances, new sacrifices might be necessary to bring a crisis to its end.[30] Violence has its limits, but at the same time it occupies its place within "sacred limits".

Norbert Lohfink, professor of Old Testament exegesis, has studied these problems thoroughly and, looking at the Old Testament writings, he comes to conclusions similar to Girard's. But he can show that there are dramatic tensions within the history and literary testimonies of Old Israel.

At the beginning Israel and its forefathers were burdened and contaminated by the sacralized killing of human beings. This was part of their cultural and religious environment. "Theological exaltation of wars and victories is not an invention of Israel . . . Stories that the 'sacred awe' was decisive during battle and that God was the one who enacted everything were at hand from its beginning, including the thought that the deity can turn in wrath against its own people".[31]

It cannot be doubted that in some of the Old Testament writings there are stories and myths about "sacred wars" led by Gor or gods in favour of their devotees, similar to those of neighbouring groups. But what is new is an immense tension between the inherited ideas and new perceptions. "While, in Isaiah 7:9, 'faith' implies renouncing the usual ways of power politics, in Deuteronomy 1:32, on the contrary, 'faith' requires the readiness to set out for violent conquering of the country".[32]

Norbert Lohfink tends to the opinion that the ban (*heraem*) hanging over the enemies at the beginning meant only "renouncing a special kind of booty on the grounds of a particular vow". Only in the accounts of the Deuteronomist about the conquest of the country was it interpreted as premeditated slaughter of whole populations willed by God. In reality it seems that this was neither a real happening nor a divine command. "In historical reality it was perhaps only the expulsion of the ruling class of Canaanite cities, the downfall of domineering societies and their political systems".[33]

An uncritical reader, used to seeing texts of the Old Testament as isolated messages and teachings, must be shocked by the Deuteronomist tradition and a whole set of theologizing systematizations which transformed the original events "into an extermination of whole populations willed by God".[34] Many Christians have not yet learned to see the Old Testament writings in the light of divine intervention and of people with a living faith, through which the fog of pagan origin was gradually dissipating, making place for saving truth and preparing for the full revelation of peace and love in Jesus Christ.

We see that in the Old Testament even well-intentioned men did project their own unredeemed experiences into the image of God. If we really succeed in seeing the historical dynamics of revelation, we can only be astonished and praise the victory of divine truth over human darkness, of love over violence. But we should also see — to our own warning — the stubbornness of men clinging to traditional ideas and myths which sacralize violence in so many forms.

If we read the Old Testament in the light of the New Testament — in the light of Jesus Christ — then we are enabled to distinguish, on one side, the mixed heritage from Israel's origins and the dangerous assimilations to its cultural and religious environment, and on the other, the dynamics of divine revelation as it was perceived and taught by charismatic bearers of this revelation.

Lohfink insists that the culmination of the revelation about peace and nonviolence in Deutero-Isaiah was not an isolated event; it was prepared in many ways and is coherent with a whole process of development. His textual critique comes to this astonishing conclusion: "In the priestly historiography war does not exist".[35] We do not find in it the slightest indication of "holy wars" and/or of divine commands to slaughter whole populations.

The stubbornness with which even very religious circles in Israel perpetuated the sacralizing of violence (found also in all the neighbouring cultures) can be understood only if we realize that the inclination to violence and to ideologies justifying violence is at the heart of the "sin of the world". It is misery from which only God's intervention can free us.

Even more shocking than the stubborn resistance of the ruling religious class to Christ's message and witness of nonviolence and peace is that the hardness of heart on this central and indicative point seeps through even among Christ's chosen disciples. René Girard finds it really "mysterious" that, faced with the absolute clarity of the gospels, the "things hidden since the foundation of the world" and revealed in Jesus Christ could remain still hidden and denied by much of Christianity up to our time.

Today Christianity, indeed, all humankind stands at the decisive crossroad. Either we let God heal us from our blindness, from ideologizing violence, and from aggression, or human violence will bring our history to its end. This awareness comes through in many Church documents on peace, from *Gaudium et Spes, Pacem in Terris,* many utterances of the last popes and, with even greater emphasis, in numerous pastoral letters of various Bishops' Conferences, especially those of U.S.A. and Germany.

The U.S. Bishops' Conference takes as point of departure for future decisions the two main traditions: the one of absolute pacifism and nonviolence and the other known as the "just-war" tradition, which intends to limit violence as much as possible. The U.S. Bishops rightly conclude that, from both traditions considered in their complementarity it follows that under the present circumstances of totally destructive weapons and strategies war must be ruled out. It can no longer be an appropriate means to restore order and defend human dignity. War has no right to exist.

The United Nations Organization has repeatedly condemned war, except in extreme situations in defence of irrenounceable rights. *Gaudium et Spes* and the latest episcopal documents speak of the right to defend these indispensable human rights. But the question arises immediately: can war be an appropriate means of defending them? Is there no other alternative than that of opposing violence with violence?·

The West German Bishops' Conference states that the talk on "just" defence has meaning only "within the context of a peace ethics which requests the firm purpose and extreme effort to avoid such a situation. Besides, in an era of weapons of mass destruction, the question about the means of defence becomes ever more burning . . . The Christian ethos of love of enemy and of non-violence must become effective also in foreign politics and in international politics'.[36]

The Dutch, Belgian, as well as the U.S. episcopates, complain that up to the present time sufficient attention has not been given to the alternative of civilian nonviolent defence. They urge that in future this must be given the highest attention.[37]

The U.S. Bishops' pastoral letter, "The Challenge of Peace", marks a turning point from which no theology of peace may turn back. "Nonviolent means of resistance to evil deserves much more study and consideration than it has thus far received . . . We urge that it be measured against the almost certain effects of a major war . . . Practical reason as well as spiritual faith demands that it be given serious consideration as an alternative course of action".[38]

This carefully prepared document shows the good results of interdisciplinary dialogue and the cooperation of many competent people. It has succeeded very well in describing the scope and spirituality of nonviolent defence.

2. *"Blessed are the peacemakers"*

Those who are seized by the peace of Christ and who preserve peace in their hearts, radiate peace, give witness to peace and cooperate as much as possible in making peace attainable, are assured of great beatitude, "They shall be called sons and daughters of God" (Mt 59). They reveal themselves as genuine brothers and sisters of Jesus Christ, Prince of Peace. They find serenity and joy in God. For them it is happiness to lead people to God's peace, and to peace among themselves. "The kingdom of heaven is theirs", for "the kingdom of God is justice, peace and joy, inspired by the Holy Spirit" (Rom 14:17).

Whoever can read the Bible and decipher the signs of the times will easily understand how, in the beatitude proclaimed for the peacemakers, all the other beatitudes and the commandment of love flow together.

Peacemakers are among those who know deeply in their hearts "their need of God" (Mt 5:3) and that peace with God, peace of heart and mind and the capacity to radiate, foster, restore peace are undeserved gifts of God, the Father of all. Peacemakers cannot even dream of having a share in the kingdom of heaven without faithful use of such gifts. They know how much they need God in order to resist temptation arising from a world full of collective egotism, lies, lust for power, lust for wealth. They want to become a leaven of peace in this world.

A commentator on the writings of the great peace researcher, C. F. von Weizsäcker, accuses him of abysmal pessimism because he has the courage to tell himself and others that humankind imprisoned in power battles, superpowers hypnotized by thirst for superiority, and persons terribly affected by the disease of peacelessness are, by themselves, absolutely unable to build a genuine peace, unable to get out of the self-made trap of mutual "deterrence". Only accidentally does the commentator mention that von Weizsäcker confesses his faith that there is a God-given possibility for humankind to be converted to the spirit and great orientations of the Sermon on the Mount.[39]

A serious peace researcher cannot allow himself the luxury of easy optimism. And a Christian cannot dare to hope for redemption from peacelessness without the Divine Redeemer. Whoever understands Gospel morality as morality of grace and graciousness, and at the same time has a deep knowledge of a success-oriented culture, with its anti-aesthetic consumers and manipulated manipulators, cannot ignore the fact that such a culture, by itself, is unable to produce a milieu where truth, justice and peace have high priority. A deep change in the hearts and minds of decisive people is absolutely necessary. We should know how much we are in need of God and of conversion to his Gospel.

Von Weizsäcker intends to promote good reasoning and discernment for the needy individual, and social therapy for healing from peacelessness. But he is right in not expecting healthy reasoning and healing power from people who are not willing to search wholeheartedly for true, healing love, including love of enemies.

Some modern people are surprised when a famous scientist, philosopher and peace researcher dares to tell people that we shall be unable to solve our tremendous political problems "as long as we are not becoming capable of a loving perception of the real needs of our fellowmen, and that this love is beyond our own efforts of will, being rather experienced as grace". All this has to do with the great vision of the first and basic beatitude and of the whole Sermon on the Mount.

To my mind, the further insight of peace researcher Weizsäcker, (criticized as "pessimist") that "a world catastrophe would be unavoidable if nobody were able to love enemies",[40] belongs to the central truth of the blest peacemakers. All this is not at all an expression of abysmal pessimism but of the courage of peace and of the strong hope to which we are entitled by the gospel of peace and the promise of God's grace.

Indeed, the gospel of peace does not first tell us that we must love our enemies but, rather, assures us that the redeemed, the true believers in the Gospel, will be enabled to join the Redeemer in that love which rescues enemies and makes them friends. The world of violence, greed and lust for power must be told that it has to go through a most depressing assessment of its own resources for peace, and that it has no reason to hope for peace while refusing the hope of the Gospel: hope in God. Inability or unwillingness to understand this is part and parcel of a peaceless, arrogant world living in radical opposition to the Gospel beatitudes.

"How blest are the sorrowful; they shall find consolation" (Mt 5:4). Indeed, people do have to pass through a phase of deep sorrow when they begin to realize that, with their ideologies of power and violence, their covetousness for greater power and economic expansion, they have gone totally astray, have even shared in the guilt of the insane threat of annihilation of humankind. If listening to the gospel of peace makes them ready to despair about their false gods and ideologies, about their reasoning imprisoned in collective and individual selfishness, then they can receive the consolation of the gospel of peace and an effective and well reasoned mission of peace.

"How blest are the nonviolent; they shall inherit the earth" (Mt 5:5). The question, "to be or not to be", is now whether or not our Planet Earth will still have any inheritors and whether humankind will have any sustaining place on earth. Ruthlessness in interpersonal relations goes hand in hand with ruthless exploitation and poisoning of our planet.

The cult of violence, the boasting about the most atrocious weapons is a deadly sickness that does not allow the human family, as one family, to possess the earth entrusted to all of us. And yet the divine promise is still with us. This is all the more clear to those of gentle spirit, who do not intend the destruction of their "enemies" but have inner strength and creative vision to save people from their enmity and make them friends. They are worthy to inherit the earth and to enjoy God's gifts, together with all their brothers and sisters. The beatitude proclaimed for the nonviolent, for those of gentle spirit, precedes the beatitude for the peacemakers. It is basic for peacemaking.

"How blest are those who hunger and thirst for justice; they shall be satisfied" (Mt 5:6). With good human and theological reason the German episcopate, in their pastoral letter, "Justice Brings Forth Peace", emphasize the inseparability of dedication to justice and to peace. But much depends on what we mean by justice. It is not a vindictive "justice", not a special justice for the wealthy and powerful, but the justice for which Christ has redeemed us: the right of all to love and to be loved in a dignifying and liberating way.

Denying justice to another person causes conflict, enmity and violence. Denying justice to the lower social classes causes violent revolution, rioting and the like. Denying to nations a just place in international relations causes war. Rollo May writes: "It is often pointed out that the Germans, in the years before 1933, were in such a state of economic hopelessness and anxiety about their future, that they succumbed to the manipulative power of Hitler".[41] The powerful nations of the First World should remember this in resolving the South-North conflict in justice and generosity.

The justice that comes from the Father is a saving justice, as revealed in the peace mission of Christ and entrusted to his disciples. It is justice offered to the poor and outcast by giving them an advance of trust, enabling them to take their part in shaping our history. Right can prevail if we are grateful for the way God deals with us sinners, offering us the chance of conversion and peace. Right can prevail if we listen to the word of Christ: "I have set you an example; you are to do as I have done for you" (Jn 13:15).

Not without intention, the beatitude for those thirsting for justice is immediately followed by the praise of mercy: "Blest are the merciful; mercy will be shown to them" (Mt 5:). Here we see the therapeutic dynamics of God's plan for salvation and peace. God sets us right again by acting in Jesus mercifully, thus teaching us the healing love without which enemies cannot become friends again, and without which humankind cannot overcome the present crisis of violence.

"Blest are those whose hearts are pure; they shall see God" (Mt 5:8). A pure heart is one that is purified by the healing and liberating love of the Redeemer. Blest is the disciple who is rescued by Christ from selfishness and group interests, from violence and lust for power. Healed of blindness, he now can discern what true love is, what it demands and what it enables us to do.

There can be no hopeful peace enterprise if we do not watch over our motives and intentions, the genuineness of our love. Are we really and fully committed to that peace which comes from God and joins people in the sight of their heavenly Father? Are we committed to that peace by which God has allowed us sinners to become his friends and children, and by which we can make our enemies partners in the cause of right, of mercy and reconciliation?

According to the Gospel, the test of the genuineness of our love is the enemy who is in need of merciful, healing love, of an advance of goodness, of patient endeavour to win him over for the common good of peace. Only Christ-like love can help adversaries in the shared effort to discover their inner powers and their opportunities for peace.

After the praise and promise of peacemakers (Mt 5:9) there follows, "Blest are those who have suffered persecution for the cause of right; the kingdom of God is theirs" (Mt 5:10). This is in the logic of the Paschal Mystery. Christ has paid the price for peace. And peacemakers should not retreat if, in the pursuit of nonviolent peacemaking and commitment to that justice which produces peace, they have to suffer. Hereby, discipleship to Christ becomes deadly serious and wonderfully blest. Before the peace-maker stands the Crucified Christ, who prays for those who have tortured and crucified him physically and psychically: "Father, forgive!".

None of the dimensions of the beatitudes may be ignored or neglected. The plan of God's peace is one and indivisible. Only through the whole spirit of the beatitudes and total commitment are we enabled to perceive the healing power of peace and pacemaking. Only thus are we among the blest peacemakers, even winning over our enemies for the peace which we know to be destined for all. For God's children it is pure bliss "to bring at least a beginning of peace into this world plagued by peacelessness".[42]

The Jewish writer Pinchas Lapide speaks of the blissful experience of those "who seek peace and pursue it" (Ps 24:14): "For it is a creative, honest toil to remove walls of distrust and to build bridges", because this means to pursue "what God does day by day, whereby he intends to attract us to follow his example".[43]

3. *Healing morals of grace and peace in a success-oriented society*

The ideological trend of our whole educational system in the Western world aims, above all, at success and measurable achievement. Success ethics, inspired by a strange Calvinistic understanding of predestination, gave a certain religious note to the tireless striving for material success, although its original starting point was the doctrine of undeserved grace. This doctrine was totally perverted at the very moment when earthly success, i.e., wealth and power so often associated with ruthless exploitation of the weak, became the sign of a person's being among the predestined ones.

In a culture wherein external achievement and success rank highest on the scale of values, man becomes insensitive to everything that is meant by grace and graciousness. He does not know the bliss of unselfish love, is deaf to the divine promise and gift of peace, and crippled in the contemplative dimension so necessary for the peace-mission entrusted to us by Christ. Herein lie many of the poisoning roots of the peacelessness which is symptomatic of a social, psychosomatic and noogenic illness. If a profound healing is not forthcoming, then the precious fruits of the Spirit —

"love, joy, peace, patience, kindness, goodness, fidelity, nonviolence and self control" (Gal 5:22) — can never prosper.

Especially in this success-oriented culture of ours, it is urgent that Christians pray perseveringly for this peace which comes from God and endows the thankful ones with the charism of peacemaking. We should always and on all occasions give thanks for the promise and gift of peace.

Preaching the gospel of peace and pleading for commitment to peacemaking, we can never emphasize enough God's own gracious initiative, his gift of peace and reconciliation. Peacefulness, dedication to the great cause of universal peace — including the readiness to suffer in pursuit of justice and peace — cannot be understood as human achievement but only as "bearing fruit in love", as eloquently described in Johannine and Pauline theology.

In this vision of faith we can gradually grasp how much the love of enemy (rescuing the enemy from his imprisonment in peacelessness) becomes the test of our gratitude for God's undeserved gift of peace and reconciliation offered to us sinners. By sin we all were God's enemies, prisoners, hopelessly sick. For all this we give thanks and glory to God in truth by reaching out to those who oppose us or have wronged us, without expecting them to take the first step.

Pinchas Lapide explains the word of the Bible, "Love your neighbour; I am the Lord": "Wherever two on earth make peace and love each other, there God is the Third in the covenant". There, God is truly honoured as Lord. The fact that God loves us sinners and calls us to holiness, to intimate friendship, gives believers the strongest motives to love their enemies and endeavour to make them friends. Those who constantly praise God for his undeserved love and his saving, healing commandment of love will come to an ever better understanding of this.

Our fellowmen, whatever their appearance of wickedness and power, are fundamentally as weak as we are, as exposed to anguish as us. They are, like us, created to the image of God; yet sick and weak, like us. This being-like-us should disarm any distrust in us; it should free us from anger and anxiety. "Then the doors of your heart will open themselves for the flow of freely offered love".

In this context, Pinchas Lapide quotes a dear friend of mine, Rabbi Joshua Heschel: "God says: 'I have created both of you to bear my image, so hatred of your neighbour is nothing less than hatred of God in disguise. By fostering grudges, calumnies, contempt against your neighbour, you do all this against the divine spark burning in his heart and granting him the nobility of true humanness".[44]

It depends much on the way we meet our neighbour, whether he will become our friend or our enemy, whether we and he discover in ourselves the good coming from God or let it atrophy. A firm fundamental option to free our neighbour from enmity, in thanksgiving for God's gratuitous love, makes us creative in discovering and promoting the good in ourselves and in them.

On the contrary, if we live only at the level of a morals of achievement and success, which has also the features of a morals of retribution, of payment in kind, we remain miserable and spread misery.

In a success-oriented society, even the psychiatrist cannot speak meaningfully on nonviolence without reminding his reader that "When it is authentic, nonviolence has a religious dimension, since by its very nature it transcends the human forms of power".[45] Only grateful persons and communities are on the wavelength of this gift and challenge of peace and nonviolence.

4. *Peace of God and reconciliation of man: confronting peaceless ideologies*

In the perspective of the history of salvation and of solidarity, a great biblical model of the peace coming from God and reconciling people is the reconciliation of Jewish and Gentile Christians in the one body of Christ, the one Church. This is an essential dimension of the Pauline gospel of peace, with far-reaching consequences for reconciled diversity in kerygma, liturgy and community-building. "Now in union with Christ Jesus, you who were far off have been brought near through the shedding of Christ's blood. For he himself is our peace. Gentiles and Jews he has made the two one, and in his own body of flesh has broken down the enmity which stood like a dividing wall between them, for he annulled the law with its rules and regulations, so as to create out of the two a single new humanity in himself, thereby making peace. This was his purpose, to reconcile the two in a single body to God through the cross, on which he killed the enmity" (Eph 2:13–16).

The Letter to the Ephesians is one great hymn of praise for this reconciliation inspiring all of life. The Letter to the Galatians draws concrete and far-reaching conclusions arising from this reconciling gospel, foreshadowed already by the faith of Abraham. All cultural, social and sexual diversities have to yield their divisiveness to the choir united in praise of the Reconciler and Redeemer. All this, in purified streams, shall flow together in order to make fruitful the work of peace. "There is no such thing as Jew and Greek, slave and freeman, male and female: for you all are one person in Christ Jesus" (Gal 3:28).

It was not at all easy for the apostolic Church to leave behind all the divisive ideologies and traditions and to draw all the wholesome conclusions from the gospel of peace and reconciliation. The Church's history is full of good initiatives but also clouded by many drawbacks which, like frost and hailstorms, set back her peace-mission in many ways.

Today the world is filled with different ideologies which block peace and cooperation among nations, social classes, and even among Christians. In the foreground is the ideological conflict between East and West. The West, proudly calling itself "The Free World" is amazingly clearsighted in discovering anti-peace ideologies in the East's Communist parties. There is, indeed, a dangerous ideology about "eternal peace" which can be expected only when all nations have been forced to accept the Communist doctrine and all Communist parties of the world abide with Moscow's interpretation of orthodox Marxist doctrine. It is a secularized rendering of false messianism, which expected the submission of all nations to Israel, the "chosen people"[46] — an ideology forcefully denounced by Christ.

On the other side, Marxists are amazingly clearsighted in discovering and unmasking the ideologies behind capitalism and hegemonism in the West, but rather blind to those which they share with private capitalism. They rightly denounce colonialism and neo-colonialism, but they do so while imposing by force and threats their ideologies on entire reluctant populations and nations. Marxists rightly denounce the ideologies behind the military-industrial complex of the West, which is greatly responsible for the

the Southern hemisphere; but they seem blind to their own military-industrial and security complex, hardly different from that of the West.

Superpowers on both sides exploit our planet to the detriment of poor nations and future generations, and both sides are accountable for increasing air and water pollution.

The peace coming from God and the reconciliation intended by the redemption must be so proclaimed and practised by Christians that all people of every socio-economic systems and culture will become self-critical and honestly join efforts against such ideologies, in order to promote the cause of peace in all its dimensions. Here is a main field for our peace-mission and the right proclamation of the gospel of peace. One of the great obstacles and handicaps — even among churchmen — is the age-old inclination to self-righteousness, which ascribes all the evil to the opponent and all the good to oneself.

If teaching peace ethics implies that we begin conversion among ourselves and focus first on ideology-criticism of our own camp, then the appeal of the German episcopate makes sense: "A peace-ethics, inspired by the directives of Christ, concedes to the other, including the opponent, the capacity for conversion and for shared learning. In this way the Christian ethos of love of enemy and of nonviolence will have its impact also on foreign politics and international politics".[47]

5. *Urgency of a synthesis between ministries of peace and of healing in today's world*

The biblical concept of peace (*shalom*), the whole gospel of peace and the signs of the times urgently call for a synthesis and synergy of peace-making and healing. There are opportunities and a budding sensitivity for this appeal. Of the biblical concept of peace, a Jewish thinker explains: "The biblical '*shalom*' means not only peace, as so many think, but above all, uninjured wholeness, compact unity, the antithesis of schizophrenia and alienation of self. Indicated is an indivisible integrity which means, from within, harmony of hearts on the way to a being-with-God, and in all directions solidarity and concord within one's nation and among all nations: expression of harmony as intended by God".[48]

To appreciate the urgency and the opportunities for an actual synthesis and synergy of dedication to peace and healing, the first requirement is a firm faith in the saving and healing power of the gospel of peace, and, second, a factual awareness of the barbaric insanity of the present arms race and the mutual threat of destruction "for security's sake".

The peace message of the West German episcopate shows fruitful attempts which call for further development. On the one hand the Bishops call for earnest self-examination and for understanding our situation as "wounded healers". They warn: "All this shows how Christians, time and again, can succumb to temptations of lust for power and violence, thus disregarding the instructions of their Lord".[48] On the other hand, they emphasize the healing and liberating power of love as the heart of our peace mission. "This love, with all its strength, will constantly try to win over the opponent to peace, discover nonviolent solutions to conflicts and offer fields of cooperation. Thus the diabolic circle of violence will be broken, its aggressivity and trend to confrontation will be dismantled".[49]

In this context, we appreciate C. F. von Weizsäcker's proposal to combine a creative love for healing the sickness of peacelessness with the promotion of a political culture which is worthy to be called "care for those not yet healed from peacelessness".[50]

Only those who have a deep faith in redemption and the peace mission of Christ and his disciples can deliver the world from the illusion that wars are unavoidable and that people must canalize their aggressivity to live peacefully. In view not only of the terrible dangers of our age but, above all, of the dynamics of salvation history, we have to proclaim wholeheartedly: "War never again! It is peace that must guide the destinies of peoples and of all mankind!".[51]

From John XXIII to John Paul II the good news resounds from St Peter's successors: "Peace is possible." Our endeavour to rid humankind from the age-old slavery of war and the ideology that wars are necessary or at least unavoidable is a fundamental option of Christian hope and healing love, in total readiness for the gospel of peace.

We can and must proclaim this gospel of peace so that we and those to whom we speak will come to an active faith in its healing power. "It is not the gospel of the reign of peace that is called to stand the test, but rather those who profess this gospel being urged to do their utmost to eliminate peacelessness among people, enmity and violence from their very roots, and this by the power of the peace entrusted to them".[52]

It is most encouraging that a Jewish believer warns Christians not to "put aside the Sermon on the Mount as obliging nothing. In a word, it is guidance for the alert conscience of all times and for all those who believe in a possible humanization of the children of Adam".[53] For me, this is simply faith in the Redeemer of humankind, and thanksgiving for his healing love and for our mission.

Clearly, education and motivation for nonviolence are central for healing and overcoming aggressiveness, hatred and enmity. Hence, special attention is now to be paid to this theme.

NOTES

26. H. Frankenmölle, *Friede und Schwert*, Mainz 1983, 166.
27. cf. Note 15. In the following pages I quote from Girard's main work, *Des choses macches depuis la fondation du monde*, Paris 1978.
28. R. Girard, *Des choses cachées*, 33.
29. Op. cit., 38.
30. Op. cit., 37.
31. N. Lohfink (ed.), *Gewalt und Gewaltlosigkeit im Alten Testament*, Freiburg im Br. 1983, 59.
32. Op. cit., 68.
33. Op. cit., 69f.
34. Op. cit., 70.
35. Op. cit., 76 and 83. The dynamics of revelation is clearly described by N. Lohfink/R. Pesch, *Weltgestaltung und Gewaltlosigkeit. Ethische Aspekte des Alten und Neuen Testaments in ihrer Einheit und ihrem Gegensatz*, Düsseldorf 1978.
36. *Gerechtigkeit schafft Frieden*, Bonn 1983, 41f.
37. Declaration of the Belgian Bishops of July 1983: "Maybe the Church of earlier times and of today should have given more emphasis to the witness of nonviolence", in: *Bischöfe zum Frieden*, Bonn 1983, 216. The Dutch Bishops, in their declaration of May 1983, are even more emphatic: "The development of methods which enable people to resist injustice and to defend themselves without using violence is in keeping with the spirit of the Gospel and may not be labelled as utopian and unrealistic", in: *Bischöfe zum Frieden*, 142.
38. "The Challenge of Peace", in: *Origins* 13 (1983), 21–22.

39. H. Theisen, "Die Theorie der Wahrscheinlichkeit des dritten Weltkrieges bein Carl Friedrich von Weizsäcker", in: *Frankfurter Hefte* 30 (1984), 33–44.

40. l.c., 43.

41. R. May, *op. cit.*, 10.

42. E. Biser, *Gedanken des Friedens*, l.c., 72.

43. P. Lapide, *Wie liebt man seine Feinde?*, Mainz 1984, 30f.

44. P. Lapide, *op. cit.*, 36.

45. R. May, *op. cit.*, 112.

46. Lately, a number of American writers have put their finger on this wound. President Truman is quoted as saying: "The atom bomb was no 'great decision' . . . It was merely another powerful weapon in the arsenal of righteousness". (John Toland, *The Rising Sun*, New York 190, 867). Gerard A. Vandenhaar (*Op. cit.*, 21f) writes about Truman (who had strong support behind him): "He wanted to use this 'artillery weapon' not only to end the war by forcing the Japanese into unconditional surrender, but also, as his Secretary of State, James Byrnes, was understood to say, 'to make Russia more manageable in Europe' ".

47. *Gerechtigkeit schafft Frieden*, Bonn 1983, 42.

48. P. Lapide, *op. cit.*, 51.

49. *Gerechtigkeit schafft Frieden*, Bonn 1983, 29 and 19.

50. C. F. von Weizsäcker, *Der ungesicherte Friede*, 54–56, 109.

51. Address of Paul VI to the U.N. General Assembly, October 4, 1965, n. 19.

52. A. Vögtle, *Was ist Friede?*, Freiburg 1983, 68f.

53. P. Lapide, *op. cit.*, 15.

CHAPTER THREE

Nonviolence at the heart of the gospel of peace

1. *Facing the destructive and sickening myth of violence*

Looking at human history and our own historical experience, we see a frightening picture of the destructive qualities and consequences of human violence. The most unhealthy and most dangerous aspect, however, is that people have so often and persistently tried to justify and even glorify their ruthless abuse of power and their cruel violence. This insanity is laid bare in the light of the gospel of peace, which denounces all these myths as lies, and offers as remedy the healing power of love, including, essentially, love of our enemies.

Time and again, modern science has approached the question of where and how peacelessness and violence got hold of men. Why do we hate each other far beyond the measure which we bring to our consciousness? "What is the allure, the fascination, the attraction of war?"[54]

The most dangerous answer comes from social Darwinism, which reached its most insane and obscene expression in national socialism: "The victor will be the one who knows best how to fight and is willed to fight". Analysing this ideology, von Weisäcker writes: "If aggressivity is part and parcel of our biological heritage, then it is easy to glorify it as heroism. . . . Peacelessness is then the mark of the healthy man, and in no need of healing."

But this interpretation of history is madness. "That animals are peaceful within their own species is not at all surprising. The amazing thing is that aggression against members of the 'own' species is so widespread among the higher species of animals and that it increases in the human species — and only there! — unto systematic killing of other people".[55]

On the basis of Darwin's main concern — survival — we should rather expect that, within a species where aggression turns against the species even unto the risk of extinction, the instinct for self-perpetuation and conservation should work for a radical change. However, for the human species, gifted with the capacity of self-knowledge and freedom, conservation is no longer just a matter of instinct. Man's responsibility is called to reflection and to meaningful canalization of the rich energies that are dissipated in aggression.

As already mentioned, René Girard tries to explain the explosive overloading of violent aggression within the human species by the rapid increase in the capacity and trend of mimesis, especially in matters of appropriation and this very aggression. So, violence against violence is not only a question of self-defence but more fundamentally of primitive mimesis.

Girard is convinced that myths and rituals from the oldest layers of history indicate that, at the height of the crises of extinction by violence, the remedy was sought and partially found in prohibitions comined with rituals which sanctioned the prohibitions. At the centre of these rituals is the idea of the scapegoat — of vicarious sacrifice. Behind it stands a confused memory of the killing of an important man at the foundation of a city or of a tribe. "In the foundation mechanism there is reconciliation around the sacrifice".

Yet, this kind of celebrating reconciliation bears in itself the germ of future explosions of violence. "This sacrifice represents at the same time something evil and something good, an aspect of peace and an aspect of violence, of life that brings death, and death that should assure life". This mythology, culminating in the memorial of foundation killing, time and again cries for the scapegoat, for the mythological denunciation of those who should be exterminated so that "people can live". "The most fantastic charges are found among groups which are captives of their own most frightening and crude forms of violence".[56]

Girard deals sharply with some of the ideas of Sigmund Freud who, in *Totem and Taboo*, explains hominization by a collective murder. By a kind of short circuit, Freud concludes that behind all hatred of the father and killing of the father, there stands in the subconscience a furious god; and Freud's remedy is to get rid of all thoughts of a God. Girard comments with some scarcasm on Freud's interpretation which, in his eyes, mixes some true points with some crazy ideas: "A furious 'father' is the last god of violence, and we can safely say so, because such a deity at the base of psychoanalytic religion is dying today anyhow".[57]

With Girard, I consider anti-Semitism and the cruel persecutions of Jews, with all their mythical "justifications", as one of the most frightening aberrations, especially insofar as Christians were involved. Such cruelty and such myths are in absolute opposition to the Christian religion of redemption. After the cross on which human atrocity killed the Redeemer, Auschwitz is the last-flame signal of degenerate mythologies of violence which sacrifice people — indeed, humanness itself — and designate whole populations and groups as scapegoats who should die so that others may live.

Is not the actual system of M.A.D. already the last cry of the violent myths of the scapegoat who must be killed so that others may live? However, the new aspect is that now whole nations, and even the whole of humankind, become hostages and scapegoats. The most virulent ideologies, which in this 20th century have been fighting each other, "are based on a kind of monstrous rationalization of sacrifice-mechanisms, tending to affirm that the entrance into paradise depends on a previous extinction or violent conversion of categories of people to whom fault is attributed".[58]

Considering the present enormous means of mass destruction and the accompanying ideological "justifications" for using them, the chances of survival for human life as we know it are becoming grim. Humankind stands at the crossroad. With prophetic anger, Girard warns that, under such historical circumstances, noncommittal talk about an ideal of nonviolence is not really helpful. "From now on we are faced with a more and more inexorable necessity. A final and irrevocable renunciation of violence imposes itself as *condicio sine qua non* of survival of humankind and of each of us".[59]

Girard is convinced that this irrevocable decision is precisely what the biblical revelation, the extreme nonviolence of Christ's dying for us on the cross, his resurrection and the signs of the times require of us. A deeper insight into all the "scapegoat" mythology enforces such a decision for those who believe in the gospel of peace. What humankind needs is a strong faith in the Redeemer and redemption, a deeper insight into redemption from violence as an integrating part, and good reasoning, which is possible for genuine believers in healthy communities of believers.[60]

2. *The dynamics of nonviolence in the light of the Gospel*

Let us now recall the beatitude of those who, renouncing violence, will inherit the earth (Mt 5:5). Bishop Klaus Hemmerle has translated the message into everyday language:

> Blest are those who pay as much attention to the interests and concerns of others as to their own: they shall foster peace and unity.
>
> Blest are those who take the first step to meet others; they shall discover that the other is much more open than it seemed.
>
> Blest are those who never lose patience; they shall always find a new beginning.
>
> Blest are those who first listen and only then speak; they shall be listened to.
>
> Blest are those who, in discussions, always discover first what is right in the contributions of others; they shall be able to integrate and mediate.
>
> Blest are those who never use their positions egotistically; they shall be met with respect.
>
> Blest are those who are never offended or disappointed; they shall create a good climate.

Peace researcher Theodor Ebert writes: "The technical skill of atomic fission has found its liberating counterpart in the social invention of nonviolent solutions of conflicts. Our faith in the love of God tells us that he will never leave us alone in situations which seem to be hopeless". He describes nonviolence, above all, in view of its scope: "The scope is to turn opponents into friends".[61]

Other peace researchers give the following description: "Nonviolence is understood as a principle of life which renounces violence as means of solving conflicts in all realms of life (in society, in the approach to nature, in interpersonal relationships and within oneself). But nonviolence is not just refusal of violence. It is at the same time the givenness of a positive strength, which creates new chances and opportunities in life and fosters those already existing".[62]

How strong the emphasis on nonviolence has become is shown in a characteristic expression in the Japanese Hierarchy's pastoral letter on peace (1983): "It is self-evident that our endeavours for peace must be nonviolent".[63] This increasing affirmation of nonviolence can be the saving turn if, with leading biblical scholars, we consider nonviolence as expression of "the praxis of the kingdom of God and as the core of the proclamation and attitude of Jesus".[64]

In recent years, more than ever in past history, biblical scholars have studied the questions around nonviolence as a central theme in the history of revelation. It is no longer just a matter of accumulating quotes from the bible; the main attention is given to the dynamics of the history of revelation culminating in Jesus Christ. Norbert Lohfink describes it with these two short sentences: "The Old Testament came from a still violent world. However, it has unmasked and denounced violence and has projected its being overcome".[65]

Today we find ourselves in a much better situation for approaching these questions than we did fifty years ago when we studied Scripture. I heard the same feeling expressed by the biblical scholar P. C. Craigie. He complained that, during his first theological studies, he did not find any response which could free him from his "theological anguish" at seeing God and war identified.[66]

We can now discover and admire the development of divine revelation and of the faith of its bearers, which perhaps on no other point is more astonishing and important than in the increasing unmasking of violence and all the lies and ideologies surrounding it. The final result is a clear orientation to nonviolence.[67] Many prayers of the Old Testament witness to the readiness to renounce any kind of vindictiveness and to let God alone be the judge. Yet, some projections of human ideas on vindictive justice into the very image of God cannot be denied.[68]

a) *The saving power of the nonviolence of the Servant of Yahweh*

The truth is emphatic: "God is the just judge. Trust and entrust your cause to him!" But the manner in which God will bring judgement and at the same time salvation has not yet been unveiled. One thing is clear: divine judgement means salvation for those who entrust themselves to God. "Violence inflicted by man on man, especially on the God-fearing, can be finally overcome only by Yahweh".[69]

In the marvellous Songs of the Servant of Yahweh, the hidden *dynamis* of God's saving justice breaks through. In the New Testament it will become a central aspect of the gospel of peace and of the writings of St Paul. Only the witness of the Servant of Yahweh, who "submitted to be struck down and did not open his mouth . . . though he had done no violence and spoken no word of treachery" (Is 53:7–9) brought forth the insight that Yahweh is able and willing to open the eyes of sinners and violent men to the fact that the violence of evildoers will be overcome as soon as they acknowledge that their wrongdoing is inhuman, is sinful. God's judgement can save not only the oppressed but even the oppressors who are converted to him and transformed.[70]

Since Jesus evidently saw himself and his mission as the fulfilment of the Servant of Yahweh prophecy, biblical scholars pay great attention to these texts of Deutero-Isaiah. What is said in these songs about violence and nonviolence belongs to the very core of the promise. "In this work, which belongs to the summit of Old Testament tradition, is presented a form of implementation of Yahweh's kingdom on earth, a form which sets new standards regarding the relation between violence and nonviolence".[71]

Reading these texts carefully, against the background of human history and particularly the history of religion outside divine revelation, one can only be amazed at the clarity and coherence with which they tell us that Yahweh does not need violence in order to establish his kingdom. His ways are not the ways of men. Indeed, the very first verse of the first of the Songs of the Servant indicates God's guarantee for the message: "Here is my servant. . . . I have bestowed my spirit upon him" (Is 42:1). Then immediately follows a message which infers the theme of nonviolent liberation: "He will not call out or lift his voice high, or make himself heard in the open street".

Ernst Haag explains: "This text, according to the Hebrew word, *s'q*, recalls the tradition of calling in the open street to the army for the Yahweh war".[72] The Servant of Yahweh does not call for destruction and vindication; he brings healing. This is indicated in the following verse: "He will not break a bruised reed, nor snuff out a smouldering wick . . . he will neither rebuke nor wound" (Is 42:3–4).

The mission of the Servant is worldwide: "I have formed you, and appointed you to be a light to all peoples, a beacon for the nations" (Is 42:6). His purpose of healing and liberation is worldwide: "to open eyes that are blind, to bring captives out of prison".

The second song gives an impressive picture of the Servant's enormous task and of seeming or temporary failures: "Once I said: 'I have laboured in vain; I have spent my strength for nothing, to no purpose" (Is 49:4). The response is solemn and dramatic: "But now Yahweh has spoken: 'It is too slight a task for you, my servant, to restore the tribes of Jacob, to bring back the descendants of Israel; I will make you a light to the nations, to be my salvation to earth's farthest bounds' " (Is 49:6).

Strongly emphasized is the amazing difference between the weakness of the means and the final result, the fulfilment of Yahweh's plan of salvation. The Servant is "one who thinks little of himself, whom every nation abhors, the slave of tyrants". But, "When they see you, kings shall rise, princes shall rise and bow down, because of the Holy One of Israel who has chosen you, and I helped you on the day of deliverance" (Is 49:7–8).

The same contrast marks the third song. On one hand there is the extreme patience in humiliation, and on the other hand Yahweh's mighty intervention: "I did not hide my face from spitting and insult; but the Lord God stands by to help me; therefore no insult can wound me" (Is 50:6–7). The main emphasis here is on the readiness of the Servant to listen kindly and to console the weary (Is 50:4) — a fundamental aspect of nonviolence in the biblical texts.

The fourth song of the Suffering Servant begins with a divine guarantee that this way leads to its purpose, although many are shocked. "Behold my servant shall prosper, he shall be lifted up, exalted to the heights. Time was when many were aghast at you" (Is 52:13–14). The way followed by the Servant contradicts the ways which men choose, even unto now. "He was despised, he shrank from the sight of men, tormented and humbled by suffering" (Is 53:5). But great is the error of those who thought that he was beaten by the Lord (Is 53:5). The Servant suffers freely, in fulfilment of his mission to establish God's kingdom of long-suffering love: "He was pierced for our transgressions, tortured for our iniquities; the chastisement he bore is health for us, and by his scourging we are healed" (Is 53:5).

Here is the clearest expression of the healing power of nonviolence, wherein the revealer and the summit is the Servant. The nonviolence by which he establishes the kingdom of God is expressed in images that can be understood by everyone. "He was afflicted, he submitted to be struck down and did not open his mouth; he was led like a sheep to the slaughter" (Is 53:7), "though he had done no violence and spoken no treachery" (Is 53:9).

Thus the age-old pattern of the "scapegoat" is reversed. What men did to the Servant is abominable. They did not act as God willed. Their act of murder had no life-giving power. People must see what a great crime they have committed. Finding a scapegoat does not bring salvation to the murderers. Healing comes from the one who, by his nonviolence and forgiving love, calls for conversion and liberation from violence. The Servant "intercedes for their transgressions" (Is 53:12), but not without calling for conversion and showing the way of peace: nonviolence.

Vernand Eller rightly concludes: "The Servant individual *does* what the servant Israel *should* do".[73] Since the mission of the Servant is universal, those who shall walk on the roads of peace and nonviolence will form the "new Israel". The great prophecy of Deutero-Isaiah, fulfilled in Jesus Christ, assures us that "the only hope for peace is in a faith that follows the ways of gentleness as well as of might".[74] The very gentleness opens the redeemed to the might of love.

René Girard is attentive to the Songs of the Servant. In the light of these texts all the myths which glorified the violent sacrifices in the history of religion are unmasked. There is a whole new perspective. The innocence of the sacrificed person is now exalted.[75] Old concepts can no longer be applied to the one who has shown the greatest love, given his life for his friends, indeed, for sinners.[76]

The Songs of the Servant become a great breakthrough for the divine revelation that God's plan of salvation intends nothing less than to rescue sinners from their violence and from all ideologies that try to justify violent sacrifices even on religious grounds.

"Modern historical critique has given attention to the four songs in themselves, and shows thereby their unity and independence from the context. This is to be highly appraised, especially since it had been unable to tell us of what their uniqueness consists. The most striking and unique aspect is the innocence of the Servant of God: that he has nothing to do with violence and no affinity whatsoever with violence".[77]

Girard is most interested in interpreting the text as a whole, in such a way that no doubt is left that it was not God who beat the Servant. "The responsibility of God is implicitly denied". Unfortunately, Girard made unnecessary trouble for himself by taking uncritically a translation of Isaiah 53:10 according to which "It pleased Yahweh to crush him through suffering".[78] The New English Bible as well as the new ecumenical German translation rightly read: "Yet the Lord took thought of his tortured servant and healed him who had made himself a sacrifice for sin".

Exactly in this sense Girard understands the gospel's account that neither God the Father nor the Son-made-Man was seeking suffering and a violent death. Indeed, Jesus did everything to win over his people for God's plan. Something quite different is that, from a certain moment, Jesus could and did foresee the clash between his absolute nonviolence and the atrocious violence which, up to that hour, was so much incarnate in this sinful world.

From his baptism in the Jordan unto his resurrection, the inspired authors of the New Testament see Jesus' mission in the light of the Songs of the Servant. The Sermon on the Mount and Jesus' emphasis on nonviolence and love of enemy cannot be fully understood without the preparation of New Testament revelation through the Old Testament, and particularly without reference to the Songs of the Servant in Deutero-Isaiah.

Reading the Sermon on the Mount in this full context, we realize that we cannot believe fully in the redemption if at the same time we declare the core orientations, the Beatitudes, mere utopia. Today many Protestant theologians criticize sharply a Lutheran doctrine which considered the Sermon on the Mount as a not-really-obliging guideline but as a sharpening of the law that must convince man — even the believer — that he cannot fulfil this law.[79] Of course, as Christians we all know that we cannot fulfil it by our own strength and that we should never dream that we have already done enough.

Rudolph Schnackenburg, in his survey of the interpretations of the Sermon on the Mount throughout history, shows us how seriously the apostolic Church was convinced that this law is truly meant as the way of life, obliging and possible through grace, possible at least in the sense of being-on-the-road and never stopping. The Church Fathers were fully aware of the intimate connections between these binding and liberating orientations and God's action in creation, providence and especially in Jesus Christ.[80] Therefore, they loved this law, written primarily in the spirit and the heart of the children of God.

Anton Vögtle writes that, in view of the Sermon on the Mount, those who believe in the Gospel "have to do their utmost to overcome interpersonal peacelessness, enmity and violence, through the power of peace given to them . . . Jesus' call to work for change in human relationships, which from their roots are characterized by violence and counterviolence, may not be abandoned".[81]

Girard's formulations concerning the healing of public life by a creative commitment to nonviolence sound much more energetic. He is convinced — and rightly so — that the main point is to show how unique and how central in the gospels is the liberation from violence and the commandment to love and to reason insofar as possible the enemies from violence and treachery. In the same manner, Heinrich Spaemann writes: "Jesus is nonviolent because God is nonviolent. God does not force, he shows trust; he sets free and guides to freedom . . . Nonviolence, just as much as poverty, belongs to the mystery of the Redeemer and redemption. The test is whether one shares in that mystery".[82]

For many people today it has become fashion to speak of the Sermon on the Mount and its core-message as "utopia". John Topel warns energetically against this. "The Sermon is necessary because its principle of love of neighbour is not, as in utopian thought, an ideal principle, but a *real* one . . . Utopias do not now exist; they are nowhere".[83] "Utopia" (*ouk — topos*: "no place") is a beautiful dream which easily invites to flight and "if only" wishfulness. The Sermon is "eutopia" (*eu — topos*: "a good place, a real place") for the redeemed in this real world of struggle between the old and the new world.

The biblical scholar, Rudolf Pesch, joins in the radical interpretation of Girard and of Raymund Schwager, professor of dogmatic theology: "As basis for their life, the followers of Jesus in the New Testament communities celebrate Jesus' death as the eschatological victory over violence. The way to overcome violence is indicated to them by discipleship . . . In the interpretation of the death of Jesus, the New Testament communities profess that God himself, in his Son, has been touched by the universal violence of humankind. God himself has broken open the devilish circle of memesis instead of reacting with a destructive judgement to the murder inflicted on his Son".[84]

Only if we grasp this truth and event most earnestly as gift and challenge in all our life can we hope to experience fully the healing power of the gospel of peace and nonviolence.

b) *The power of love in healing enemies*

The redeeming love revealed in Jesus Christ is essentially an all-embracing love that also rescues and heals the enemy from violence and hatred, and wins him over for God's reign of love. God does not beat back. In his Son, Jesus, he suffers the beating which the sinner has deserved. "By his wounds we are healed".

This is a central theme of Pauline theology and kerygma. God's mighty love, which redeems and heals enemies to bring them home into his kingdom, unmasks the powerlessness and sickness of vindictive "justice", which is vindictive lovelessness acting under the guise of justice. This truth of the healing love of God may never be treated marginally in Christian ethics. It is not sufficient to add it to an ethics built on totally different structural principles.[85]

Conversion to the neighbour in forgiving, liberating, healing love is a distinctive teaching not only of the Sermon on the Mount but of the whole New Testament. Those whose life is marked by praise of God's healing and saving love and mercy will embrace a healing love of enemy as sign of entering into God's kingdom, and give it high place in all their relationships. "The experience of the magnanimous and forgiving love of the Father, who gives the sinner an advance, should motivate people and set them afire to share this love and peacemaking".[86]

The victory of Jesus' reconciling and redeeming love was won, in the midst of a hostile and extremely violent world, by his prayer on the cross "Father, forgive!". Jesus, who has shown this love to us, who by our sins were his enemies, does not invite us to dream about an easy-going love in a perfect, utopian society, but by his very love and graciousness calls us to enter with him into the "eutopia", the "good place", of God's kingdom.[87] By fully accepting this call we are the realists in the midst of absolute reality. Thus, and only thus, in union with Christ, we offer the world an idea of true faith in the God who is love and compassion.[88]

If we continue along this road, whatever our handicaps and external obstacles may be, we have a good chance to heal those who up to now were not able to love because they had not yet received enough genuine love. Thus they can join us at the banquet of peace and love.

Healing love of enemy is an "aggressive" and strong medicine. taminate or harm us with their violence, is the supreme form of love of neighbour in the very footsteps of Jesus. It is true that this kind of love brought Jesus to the cross, but it is precisely there that he has proved the full extent not only of his love but of his might. Pinchas Lapide writes of a rabbi who asked the question: "Who is the mightiest in the country?", and replies: "He who wins the love of his enemy!"[89] Is it not the greatest honour and challenge to be invited by the Saviour to join him in this mighty love?

Healing love of enemy is an "aggressive' and strong medicine. It treats not only external symptoms but intends to heal from within, from the very roots. This powerful love was the core of Martin Luther King's message. Time and again he assured the oppressors that whatever they might do to his people, they would receive back love until the shared victory of peace and reconciliation in justice.[90]

Such perseverance and coherence is grace; grace that enables believers to realize their inner strengths and the nearness of the Saviour. Psychic and spiritual energies will be nourished by the clear vision of perspectives and proportions. In comparison with Christ's own victorious love for us as well as for our opponents most human conflicts and difficulties weigh very little. But great is the weight of the love of the disciples who faithfully join Christ and the Father, who invites sinners (enemies) to become friends, sharers of his blissful love. God himself works in and through these loving disciples.

c) *Discernment of the Spirit*

In Luke's gospel, immediately after summing up the ways leading to and away from salvation (the four "How blest!" and the four "Alas!"), Jesus says, "But to you who hear me I say: Love your enemies; do good to those who hate you; bless those who curse you; pray for those who treat you spitefully. When a man hits you on the cheek, offer him the other cheek too; when a man takes your coat, let him have your shirt as well" (Lk 6:28–29). This nonviolent approach, while taking the side of the poor and denouncing the oppressor (cf. Lk 6:20–26) marks the true disciples of Christ and their affirmation of the great commandment: "If you love only those who love you, what credit is that for you? Even sinners love those who love them . . . But you must love your enemies and do good . . . Be compassionate as your Father is compassionate" (Lk 6:32–36).

Through the nonviolent love of Christ Crucified, the Father has revealed his compassionate love for us sinners and his design to make us his children, like him in this same compassionate love for enemies. By justification through grace and by faith, this compassionate and reconciling love of the Father becomes the inner law written in our hearts, the mark of the redeemed.

Nonviolence in this total dimension is the fruit of the Holy Spirit, and thus becomes also a decisive sign for discernment of the Spirit (cf. Gal 5:13–22). Everything that characterizes treachery and violence is described as harvest of incarnate selfishness (of "flesh"): "Quarrels, a contentious temper, envy, jealousies . . . Those who behave in such a way will never inherit the kingdom of God" (Gal 5:20–21). "The harvest of the Spirit is love, joy, peace, patience, kindness, goodness, fidelity, gentleness and self-control" (Gal 5:22). All these qualities are indispensable for the healing power of nonviolence.

Rudolf Pesch sees a certain indifference towards nonviolence, a refusal of a firm option for it, as a serious question-mark about our faith, at least understood as fundamental option. "Are we afraid that the solution offered by God, the very way of Jesus, might not be true? Are we nurturing distrust towards God, towards Jesus Christ? Are we really believers?"[91]

Norbert Lohfink sees communities of Christians, faithful to the biblical models, as convincing alternatives to a society marked by violence.[92] Martin Luther King, in his nonviolent campaign for brotherhood among all peoples, eloquently described nonviolence as a distinctive sign of faith in the way of Christ. He reminds us that the very weapons of peace correspond to the quality of peace, of reconciliation, of love. He appeals to the downtrodden and outcasts not to degrade themselves by hating their opponents or oppressors. He is convinced that thus, and only thus, can all the world realize that unarmed love is the mightiest power on earth.[93]

Nonviolent action can be a distinctive sign of believers only to the extent that it avoids every trace of rage or grudge, as well as of a passive pacifism that shrinks back from co-responsibility in the world. Hence, we have to take a close look at the new "weaponry" of the gospel of peace, of love of enemy, and at the same time make sure that there is no touch of fanaticism or any kind of attitude which marked the so-called "holy wars".

3. *The new "weapons" of peace*

The dramatic development of divine revelation from when Yahweh began to manifest himself to the forefathers of the tribes which were later called Israel ("people of God") spans the time from tribal fighting and the atrocities of the "Yahweh war" — as interpreted by the Deuteronomist school — with the destruction of whole populations, unto the peace-revelation in the healing, nonviolent, patient love of Jesus. Looking at him, we speak, with Paul, of the "new weapons" of nonviolent commitment, as probed by prophets like Mahatma Gandhi and Martin Luther King.

Gandhi concentrates on two key concepts of his message and his experience: *satyagraha* and *ahimsa. Satyagraha* means the strength of trust in the might of truth and in the honest search for truth, done in love. *Ahimsa* is the irrevocable fundamental option to treat all living beings, but especially human beings, in the kindest way our conscience can conceive. A *Satyagrahi* is a man or woman who is committed to the cause of truth and love, justice and peace, and determined to use only the means of nonviolent love and truthfulness in all situations.

Gandhi's *satyagraha* norms can be counted as among the new weapons of peace and justice:

Let *ahimsa* guide all your thoughts and endeavours!
Identify yourself in love with those whom you have to oppose!
Your fight may not be primarily against something but rather for a positive purpose!
Offer your adversary an advance of trust! Make the first step!
Don't judge your opponent or anyone else harder than yourself!
Be ready for an open-ended compromise!
Do not kill!
Don't force your opponent, help him change his heart, win him for the good!
Fight against injustice and untruthfulness but never against persons!
Don't take advantage of the weaknesses of your opponent!
Never provoke your opponent!
Don't haggle! Don't make yourself dependent on help from outside!
Be willing to make sacrifices!
Try to understand the viewpoint of your opponent!
Don't hide your intentions!
Be loyal wherever you can! Never commit sabotage!
Avoid cowardice as much as violence![94]

More decisive and more eloquent than these formulated principles is Gandhi's life-long faithfulness to his option and to the ever-growing deepening of spirituality rooted in faith. Not less than the Baptist preacher, Martin Luther King, Gandhi took his inspiration from the Sermon on the Mount, from the whole New Testament, and above all from the example of Christ.

The vocabulary of the Letter to the Ephesians is somehow reminiscent of the Old Testament "Yahweh war" language. However, the whole phrasing is a quite different approach: a battle fought in a new spirit and with totally different armament. We find here a whole programme for spiritual transarmament: "Find your strength in the Lord, in his mighty power. Put on the armour which God provides, so that you may be able to stand firm against the devices of the devil . . . Stand firm I say. Fasten on the belt of truth; for coat of mail put on integrity, to give you firm footing; and with all these, take up the great shield of faith, with which you will be able to quench all the flaming arrows of the evil one. Take salvation for helmet; for sword take that which the Spirit gives you — the word that comes from God" (Eph 6:10–17).

Without the imagery of the "Yahweh war", Paul gives the same guidance in plain talk in the Letter to the Romans: "Never pay back evil for evil . . . Do not let evil conquer you, but use good to conquer evil" (Rom 12:17–21). Paul is much concerned to base his doctrine on nonviolent battle, on the reign of love in faith. For this the words of the Letter to the Ephesians are characteristic.

a. *"Fasten on the belt of truth"*

Paul speaks here of truth in the same sense as the gospel of John. Truth has a liberating and healing power if we listen to him who *is* Truth, keep him in our mind, treasure up his words, pondering them and putting them faithfully into practice (cf. Jn 8:31–32). The basic and all-embracing truth taught by Jesus is: "God is love". And this love has revealed its countenance in Jesus Christ.

This truth demands and produces in the faithful disciple purity of intention, honesty, transparent veracity in dedication to what is good, right and honest, and what fosters peace.

Careful analysis of the Old and New Testaments makes evident the relationship between violence and treachery on the one hand, and on the other, between dedication to truthfulness and peacefulness. The core-message about the Servant of Yahweh is: "he had done no violence and spoken no word of treachery" (Is 53:9). Jeremiah tells us about violent oppressors: "Their houses are full of fraud, as a cage full of birds" (Jer 5:27). He laments for Jerusalem: "Violence and outrage echo in her streets; sickness and wounds stare me in the face" (Jer 6:7). Mourning the wounds of his people, Jeremiah sees everywhere the association of violence with lie. "Lying, not truth, is master in the land . . . they have trained their tongues to lies. . . . Wrong follows wrong, deceit follows deceit" (Jer 9: 2–6).

"Lie draws after itself violence as means for the self-assertion of the sinner and for the oppression of fellowmen. Perverting truth, the liar calls 'order of peace' what in reality is dominion of injustice and violence. Treachery and violence are two aspects of sin".[95] The violent man trains even his own thinking; he does violence to his thought, deceiving himself and others. But the thicker the treachery and deceit grow, the more difficult it becomes to free oneself and others from the snares of violence and oppression.

Violence produces ideologies. Violent men are slaves of falsehood and self-deception. Inevitably a violent culture produces not only a wrong concept of man but also projects its ideologies and violence into the image of God. Think, for instance, of the destructive image of man and of God behind the politics of apartheid in South Africa. It cannot be denied that there is religiosity among adherents and promoters of apartheid, but the very nature of such religiosity consolidates the regime of violence and oppression. These people sing the *Our Father* in their places of worship, but the ideology of apartheid and its terrible applications belie each of the words of "Our Father". Its meaning has been violated. No wonder that Gandhi, who started his prophetic mission in South Africa, gives such pre-eminence to the "belt of truth", to *satyagraha* (strength of truth and truthfulness, which must include constant self-examination)!

Among sinful human beings violence itself calls for violence, for mimesis. It contaminates, clouds man's rationality, makes people sick in their hearts and in their heads. As long as the opponents are ensnared in violence, the mechanisms of mimesis constantly drive people into the darkness of treachery and self-deception. An essential part of this whole mechanism is the production of distorted images of the foe. The bedeviled enemy thus "justifies" the violence and lies as being part of a kind of "holy war". In order to enter into the kingdom of redeeming love and peace one has to get rid of the vicious circle of violence and lies. We need "the belt of truth".[96]

The killing of prophets goes always hand in hand with self-justification by a whole system of lies and self-deception. And although people entangled in this system may vocally condemn the killing of earlier prophets, fundamentally this is done in such a way as to justify one's own violent design to do away with uncomfortable prophets.

Faced with religious leaders who were already planning to do away with him, Jesus tried to help them to discover their diabolic entanglement with violence and untruthfulness: "Your father is the devil, and you choose to carry out your father's desires. He was a murderer from the beginning, and is not rooted in truth; there is no truth in him. When he tells a lie he is speaking his own language, for he is a liar and the father of lies" (Jn 8:44).

Girard writes that "Satan is a name for the whole mimetic process" — namely, of the contamination and ensnarement in violence and lie. "Strange, there is the urge to kill in order not to know oneself to be a murderer. . . . Man is always more or less a violent denial of his violence. Contrary to the religion that comes from God, man-made religion has a lot to do with this mechanism".[97]

A classical example of this terrible game is the murder of Stephen (Acts 7:51–58) which, in its feedback of lie and violence, was so similar to the murder inflicted on the Son of Man. Stephen's murderers are unwilling and somehow unable to listen to the real story of murders perpetrated against the prophets: "They gave a great shout and stopped their ears. Then they made one rush at him" (Acts 7:57).

The nonviolent acceptance of death by the prophets, and especially by *the* prophet, Jesus Christ, and his martyrs, is the healing and liberating reverse of the murderous reign of hatred, violence and lie. The witness to truth and love is able to unmask the causes of humanity's hopeless entanglement in suffering caused by hunger and misery, and even more to lay bare "all the efforts to justify these immeasurable sufferings of misery and war as if they were inevitable by-products of development".[98]

Nonviolence implies and requires not just any kind of truth, but a radical commitment to the central truth — God's healing, saving and liberating truth — and a constant effort to come to deeper insights and greater discernment of what is genuine love, coming from God and leading to the kingdom of his love. It is this fundamental option and dedication to the supreme truth and its revelation that enable people to discover the good in their opponents and "to find a common basis for solving conflicts".[99]

I do not deny that such a commitment can be possible where faith in Jesus Christ and even faith in the God of revelation is present only in the form of "analogy of faith". But we can truly grasp this vision of biblical nonviolence only in the light of Jesus Christ, "who is our peace" and assures us that "I am the truth and I am life" (Jn 14:6). Jesus himself, by his example, his word, his whole life and his death, teaches what peace and peace-making is. From him we learn the language of redeemed and healing truth in love.

We can remain with Jesus on the road of truth only as long as we refuse to respond to evil with evil, ready to try to overcome evil by doing good.

b. *"For coat of mail put on integrity"*

Justice, which we consider an essential part of the armour of peace, is that saving justice which, in the image and likeness of God's own saving justice, breathes love and compassion. We have to avoid the kind of justice that somehow remains in the vicious circle of mimesis, of vindictiveness, greed or lust for power. The nonviolent follower of Christ has "hunger and thirst to see right prevail" (Mt 5:6). He looks for that justice of which Jesus speaks: "Unless your justice is far better than that of the Pharisees and the doctors of law, you can never enter the kingdom of heaven" (Mt 5:20). Martin Buber comes close to this vision, which already shines through in the Old Testament: "I have to resist the evil in myself and also the evil in the world. I can only try to do so not through violence. I do not opt for violence".[100]

"True peace-making must begin by breaking down the walls of hostility in our own hearts".[101] This will not be possible unless we are willing to accept silently some offences and injustices to our own interests, as long as this silent acceptance harms no one else or the credibility of our commitment to justice and peace. But we shall never desert the poor, the downtrodden, wherever we are able to help.

Christ, who is nonviolence incarnate, brings to completion the prophetic tradition of uncovering violence, oppression and lie wherever this harms people and contradicts the kingdom of God. We are not allowed to abandon the world to evil. And this implies also that we do not abandon evildoers to their downfall. With the armour of integrity we shall try to heal them from their blindness, shake their conscience, rescue them from hatred and enmity, and thus invite them to the banquet of the final victory of saving justice and healing love.

Without this dynamic of integrity, nonviolence would perish in the emptiness of passivity. Our own wholeness and integrity are at stake. We cannot breathe peace in a poisoned environment if we refuse our co-operation in healing it.

Solidarity of salvation, authentic love of neighbour and of self oblige us to make the fullest possible use of the armour of peace "to defeat evil" (Rom 12:21). This means also an ongoing effort to awaken the poor from their lethargy, in such a way that the process of nonviolent transformation works in the hearts of the oppressors as well as in the poor and in the improvement of socio-economic conditions.[102]

Gandhi, Martin Luther King and other pioneers of nonviolent liberation have understood well the Gospel's interpretation of love of enemies (as well as of friends) as the mightiest attack on oppression, lies and injustice. "Nonviolence means neither negligent tolerance nor intolerant enforcement".[103] This offensive by peaceful healers uses all the "weapons" of peace offered by Jesus Christ, including the readiness to suffer rather than to inflict suffering on others. Nobody — neither the oppressed nor the oppressors — should suffer unnecessarily. Nevertheless, there is suffering inherent in the process of healing.

Having renounced any kind of vindictiveness and grudge, peacemakers will find ways to help oppressors to realize the extent of their enslavement to egotism and unjust structures, and to discover their inner powers for healing and for reconciliation with those who had previously been oppressed.

c. *"Let the shoes on your feet be the gospel of peace"*

The way Christ calls to the great peace-mission is altogether different from the recruitments of the Old Testament "Yahweh war" and the medieval crusades. Christ invites us to follow him on the road of the cross. There is no other way to discover and experience the healing power of nonviolence than by the path marked by the Paschal Mystery of suffering, death and resurrection. "The followers of Christ in New Testament communities celebrate, as the foundation of their life, the death of Christ as the eschatological victory over violence. The very discipleship shows the road. Let us try to understand the death of Christ as the hour of birth of a new nonviolent society of the people of God in the New Covenant".[104]

The gospel of peace, lived in selfless love for God and people, is worth any sacrifice, even the greatest. Lapide quotes from a letter written by Gandhi in 1939 to the German Jews, a message which best reveals the spirituality of this prophet of nonviolence: "I would challenge Hitler's hangman to kill me or take me to prison. . . . This would be a religious resistance against the godless rage of dehumanized creatures".[105]

Had Christians been raised in a spirit of nonviolent resistance and creative liberty, less drastic means might have served to prevent the holocaust. For instance, on the day on which Hitler ordered all Jews to wear on their clothes the distinctive sign of the "Star of David", all believers, all dedicated Christians should have worn this same sign. It would surely have been a risk, but not at all disproportionate to the purpose. Let us remember that Christ's sacrifice was the manifestation of an all-embracing solidarity.

Those committed to active, creative nonviolent adherence to the gospel of peace must be prepared for actions like the ones described in the book of Wisdom, where violent people say: "The very sight of him is an affliction to us, because his life is not like other people's, and his ways are different. He is a living condemnation of all our ideas. . . . Outrage and torture are the means to try him with, to measure his forbearance and learn how long his patience lasts" (Wis 2:13–20).

Christ has shown that nonviolence is strength and perseverance in love, not at all weakness. René Girard considers the commitment to Christ in nonviolent and creative love for enemies as an authentic confession of faith in Christ, the Son of Man and the Son of God. "Jesus is the unique man who fulfilled the purpose willed by God for all humanity, the only man on earth who had no affinity whatsoever with violence". I agree with Girard's concern that this redemptive uniqueness of the Son of God may not be darkened by theories similar to those of sacrifices in man-made religions which projected human violence onto the image of God, and thereby found a "justification" — although a limited one — for their violence.

Jesus' death was not a necessity arising from a vindictive justice of God. "When the completion (of Jesus' mission) on earth unavoidably involved death, it was surely not because the Father, on the ground of sacrificial reasons, had decided it. Neither the Son nor the Father should be questioned about the causes, but man, all of humanity".[106] Jesus has revealed the true image of the Father by his whole life, and interpreted it in the word: "Go and learn what the text means, 'I require mercy, not sacrifice' " (Mt 9:13; cf. Hos 6:6).

We give witness to mercy, as the Father has revealed it in his Son and as the Son has revealed it in his redemptive deeds and sufferings, when we bear the burden of the poor, when we heal and reconcile people, when we fight against injustice and make such sacrifices as must be made if we are also to rescue the exploiters and oppressors from their injustices and violence. "Why? Because Jesus does not just teach a doctrine of forgiveness; he has lived the praxis of forgiveness unto the end".[107]

"Vicarious suffering" in Jesus and his followers is not a kind of pay-off on a debt required by vindictive justice; it is the promptings of God's own work, the test of long-suffering love for the liberation of violent and sinful men from their sin, from lie, violence and oppression. Suffering is not to be sought for itself but has to be taken up in the troublesome process of breaking the vicious circle of enmity and violence. Our commitment to nonviolent and healing liberation is God's work if it conforms with Christ's work of redemption. "True, he died on the cross in weakness, but he lives by the power of God; and we who share his weakness shall, by the power of God, live with him in your service" (2 Cor 13:4). "We have been treated like sheep for slaughter — and yet, in spite of all, overwhelming victory is ours through him who loved us" (Rom 8:37).

The tireless apostle of nonviolence, James W. Douglas, consistently points to the mystery of the cross, the victory of love, and the discipleship whereby, through the power of the Spirit, Christ's followers join Christ in both suffering and glory. "The logic of nonviolence is the logic of the crucifixion, and leads the man of nonviolence into the heart of the suffering Christ".[108]

The fruitfulness of this generous love implies the risk of temporary unsuccess due to obstacles already in place. Nonviolence never forces these, but rather appeals to people's innermost freedom. The fruit comes, as in Jesus' work, after a chain of seeming failures. "The effectiveness of nonviolence is ultimately an open tomb which few men seem able to envision as the culmination of the suffering history in which they are involved".[109]

Since the ministry of nonviolent peacemaking is so fundamentally connected with the cross of Christ and his resurrection, it is a privileged sign of faith in the Paschal Mystery, trust in God and redeemed love in Christ. This faith lets us hope and trust. "The patient gentleness of long-suffering, nonviolent people is given greater might than all the most atrocious weapons on earth".[110]

d. *"Able to quench all the flaming arrows of the evil one"*

Paul's Letter to the Ephesians inspires the absolute trust that those dedicated to the gospel of peace and nonviolence are able, by the "shield of faith . . . to quench all the flaming arrows of the evil one" (Eph 6:16). The same theme is found even more concretely in the Letter to the Romans: "Never pay back evil for evil . . . If possible, so far as it lies with you, live at peace with all men. My dear friends, do not seek revenge . . . If your enemy is hungry, feed him; if he is thirsty, give him a drink; by doing this you will heap live coals on his head. Do not let evil conquer you, but use good to defeat evil" (Rom 12:17–20).

The "live coals" are the collected energies of generous and creative love by which the vicious circle of revengeful mimesis and hatred is broken. In the same sense, the first letter of Peter warns: "Do not repay wrong with wrong, or abuse with abuse; on the contrary, retaliate with blessing, for a blessing is the inheritance to which you yourselves have been called" (1 Pet 3:9). Only by this creative way of rescuing enemies from their enmity can lambs remain lambs among wolves and even hope to transform wolves into lambs (cf. Lk 10:3).

Nonviolence, which has its ground and roots in God, trusts that in the other, too, there is the germ of life which responds to the living God, the Nonviolent, just as the germ grain reacts to the light of the sun".[111]

A champion of nonviolence can deal with violent men because he trusts that, when kindly helped, they will discover the goodness in themselves and will long for peace. The last Song of the Servant speaks of the astonishment of those who having gone astray in violence and lie, had despised the Servant for his nonviolence but now realize that, through his wounds, he brings healing (Is 53:1–10). Through this saving justice he does wonders in conversion: "So shall he, my servant, justify many" (Is 53:11). Conversion to the Servant's nonviolence is the sign that, through his scourging, he has brought healing to many (Is 53:5).

We like to hope that one day the whole pastoral ministry, fully dedicated to the gospel of peace and nonviolence, will be marked by the faith and confidence of Gandhi: "It is an article of faith that no man has fallen so low that he cannot be redeemed by love".[112] Imagine what miracles of healing and conversion would occur if not only a few giants but all believers would be inspired and filled with such faith, and act accordingly! They would indeed be able to "quench all the flaming arrows of the evil one". The reaction of Saul, who seemed to be hardened in his enmity, is illuminating. When David spared his life, Saul said: "The right is on your side, not mine; you have treated me well, I have treated you badly. Your goodness to me this day has passed all bounds" (1 Sam 24:17–18).

4. *Is the calling to nonviolence an absolute?*

The New Testament prohibits not only revenge but any form of vindictive justice, any grudge. Love of enemy is not just a divine commandment for all; it is the heart of God's own economy of salvation, fully manifest in Jesus Christ. Consequently, it is a central dimension of discipleship in the footsteps of Jesus and in the image and likeness of the Father. "Life in Jesus Christ" is unthinkable without an active and creative love of enemies, with the hope to rescue them and reconciliate them.

It is a sad misunderstanding to think that biblical nonviolence means simply leaving evil and evil people alone in order not to get entangled, injured or contaminated by them. For a while Reinhold Niebuhr was a spokesman for a similar pacifism. A reason might have been his extreme pessimism about culture, while focusing one-sidedly on individual conversion. He called the ethics of Jesus "an impossible possibility". I can agree with him that nonviolence, in its various dimensions, is impossible to the unredeemed person. But I hold that it is possible to those who firmly believe in the Redeemer of the world and trust in God's grace.

Within the "law of faith and grace" love of enemy is an absolute command. Hence, I protest when Niebuhr concludes: "The law of love, in fact, is absolute and uncompromising in commanding 'non-resistance to evil' ".[113] On the contrary, love of neighbour, in its distinctive Christian form of love of enemy, demands the strongest possible resistance to evil, a persevering effort to rescue evil-people, enemies, from hatred, enmity and any similar sin. Christian nonviolence is the opposite of passive acceptance of evil. It aims, rather, at the victory over evil with the armament of peace.

The gracious calling to nonviolent liberation of enemies addresses each disciple of Christ and every community. For believers, this command is absolute and uncompromising. According to their opportunities and inner powers — which grow in the process of involvement — they can and must break the vicious circle of harmful mimesis, of paying back evil for evil, offence for offence.

The same commandment obliges also in respect of the mission of Christians to be the yeast in the dough, to make visible the kingdom of God in the social sphere. "This command of Jesus is absolute and tolerates no restriction by utilitarian consideration. Jesus tells us: 'Whoever confronts you with inimical intention shall meet your love and your intercession' ".[114] However, this is not a world-imminent maxim, a recipe for governing worldly affairs; but, it has much to do with the way of God governs his world: "But I tell you: love your enemies and pray for those who persecute you; only so can you be children of your heavenly Father, who makes his sun rise on good and bad alike, and sends the rain on the honest and the dishonest. . . .There must be no limit to your goodness, as your heavenly Father's goodness knows no bounds" (Mt 5:44–48)

For believers, God's plan in governing and saving his world, humankind, is a gift to be gratefully received and admired and an obligatory goal to strive for. The fact that even fervent believers and communities can approach it only gradually and discover only step by step all the implications does not at all mean that it is just just a matter of a virtue going beyond what is commanded or required. It is a central goal-commandment for everyone in one's interpersonal relationships and community life, and finally also for one's mission to be salt for the earth and light to the world (cf. Mt 5:13–6). The whole world should benefit by the gospel of peace through the example and commitment of Christians to overcome the curse of violence.

Add to these abiding perspectives of the New Covenant the facts of the present historical hour when, for all of humanity, it is so terribly urgent to recognize the only saving alternative to violence. However, we can speak of witness only when it is supported by an illusionless readiness to suffer. Important as the witness in itself might be, "it does not dispense us from the task of helping the majority, who are not yet ready to follow the example, to find an acceptable way".[115] While leaving no doubt about the goal, there is need for great patience and tireless common effort to find, time and again, the best possible approximation.

I can agree with the way Valentin Zsifskovits expresses the tension and dynamics: "The courageous love implied in nonviolence is one of the *radical commands* of the New Testament which proclaim the coming of the kingdom of God. Man has to orient himself to this sublime goal during his earthly pilgrimage. But in this time of tension between the 'already' and the 'not yet', the Bible already indicates that this tireless striving can be accompanied by approximations implying open-ended compromises and compelling steps in the right direction. In an imperfect world this should help man to keep firmly on his way towards the goal. . . . However, violence remains an evil, although in cases of self-defence it might be accepted as a means to prevent even greater evils".[116] The last sentence is problematic, at least if one recurs to such violence without having honestly and courageously probed the creative energies of nonviolent commitment to the cause of justice and peace. Everything has to be done to prevent the sad case of having to use violence as a last resort.

But despite all our experience of tension in this year of "already" and "not yet", "we must never degrade the biblical offer and command of peace as mere utopia, or interpret it into a mere promise for the life after death. The offer stands firm and obliges . . . This has consequences for personal life and for political action, which must not be repressed with the excuse that reality is hard".[117]

NOTES

54. R. May, *op. cit.*, 174. On the meaning, spirituality and practice of nonviolence see: M. K. Gandhi, *An Autobiography: The Story of My Experience with Truth*, Boston 1957; V. Mekty, *Mahatma Gandhi and His Apostles*, New York 1980; L. Fischer, *The Life of Mahatma Gandhi*, London 1982; M. L. King, *Strive Toward Freedom*, New York 1958; Id., *The Trumpet of Conscience*, New York 1967; Id., *Strength to Love*, Glasgow 1978; P. Regamey OP, *Non-Violence and the Christian Conscience* (with a preface by Thomas Merton), London 1966; W. R. Miller, *Nonviolence: A Christian Interpretation*, New York 1964; J. W. Douglas, *The Non-Violent Cross. A Theology of*

Revolution and Peace, London 1968; D. Berrigan, *No Bars to Manhood*, Garden City 1970; Id., *Love, Love at the End*, New York 1971; T. Merton, *Faith and Violence. Christian Teaching and Christian Practice*, Notre Dame, 3rd ed. 1976. The newest literature on this subject in French, German, Italian and Spanish is immense, but little attention has been given so far to the perspective of "healing power".

55. C. F. von Weizsäcker, *Der ungesicherte Friede*, 38 and 41.

56. R. Girard, *op. cit.,* 112. R. May (*op. cit.*, 200) comes close to Girard's vision when he writes about pathological forms of "innocence": "Is not innocence curiously bound up with murder in the ritual sacrifice in practically all cultures?"

57. R. Girard, *op. cit.*, 106.

58 *Op cit.*, 151. The scapegoat mechanism of which Girard writes is people's projection of their own evil trends as expressed in the myths of the dragon or the Sphinx, which request "sacrifices". Rollo May shows the way of liberation for both individuals and groups: "The dragon or the Sphinx in me will often be clamouring and sometimes will be expressed — but I ought to do my best to accept it as part of myself rather than to project it on you" (*op. cit.*, 255). Every person and group should be constantly aware "that good and evil are present in all of us". Such consciousness "prohibits anyone from arrogance" (*Op. cit.*, 239).

59. *Op. cit.*, 160.

60. It is heartening to see how strong an echo the publications of René Girard are finding, thus increasing the interdisciplinary research about violence and nonviolence, including the various branches of theology. Cf. N. Lohfink (ed.), *Gewalt und Gewaltlosigkeit im Alten Testament*, Freiburg 1983. The whole book deals with the challenge coming from Girard, and reactions of biblical scholars; pp. 245–247: literature around the publications of R. Girard. Similar urgent language is used by Jonas Salk, the developer of polio vaccine. He calls for active immunization against violence. "I think that goodness and nobility are genetically inscribed, but they need to be evoked".

61. T. Norbert, "Soziale Verteidigung", in: *Evangelische Kommentare* 17 (1984), 331–333. The article is just one of the numerous responses of peace researchers who give great praise to the pastoral letter of the U.S. Bishops on the challenge of peace.

62. K. Lange-Feldhahn / U. Jäger, *Alternative Sicherheitskonzepte*, Tübingen 1983, 75. For a comprehensive bibliography on nonviolence, see: Gewaltfreiheit, *Verein für Friedenspädagogik*, Tübingen 1983.

63. *Bischofe zum Frieden*, Bonn 1983.

64. H. Frankenmölle, *Friede und Schwert; Frieden schaffen nach dem Neuen Testament*, Mainz 1983, 132.

65. N. Lohfink, "Das Alte Testament und die Entlarvung der Gewalt", in: N. Lohfink / R.Pesch, *Weltgestaltung und Gewaltlosigkeit. Ethische Aspekte des Alten und Neuen Testaments in ihrer Einheit und ihrem Gegensatz*, Düsseldorf 198, 61.

66 P. C. Craigie, *The Problem of War in the Old Testament*, Grand Rapids, 1978, 106.

67. Cf. the impressive bibliography on this theme in: N. Lohfink (ed.), *Gewalt und Gewaltlosigkeit im Alten Testament*, 225–245.

68. Cf. L. Ruppert, "Klagelieder in Israel und Babylonien — verschieuene Deutung", in: N. Lohfink (ed.), *op. cit.*, 111–158, specially 150f.

69. *Op. cit.*, 156.

70. *Op. cit.*, 156f.

71. E. Haag, "Die Botschaft vom Gottesknecht: Ein Weg zur Überwindung der Gewalt", in: N. Lohfink (ed.), *op. cit.*, 159–213, quote 159.

72. *Op. cit.*, 202.

73. V. Eller, *War and Peace*, 100.

74. *Op. cit.*, 96.

75. R. Girard, *op. cit.*, 162, 168, 170ff.

76. R. Girard has received some sharp criticism for his non-sacrificial interpretation of the suffering and death of the Servant, indeed, of Jesus. However, he does not really fight against the Christian concept of sacrifice but against the application of the old dangerous myths and ideologies. We need a new language to proclaim the astonishing newness of Christ giving himself up. Without contradicting Girard we can say with John Howard Yoder: "As Cain's fratricide is prototypical of the rebellion of the race (1 Jn 3:11), so Christ's sacrifice for others is a model of our community love (3:16)". (Yoder, "Thou shalt not kill", in: *Interpretation* 34 (1980), 397f). Cf. J. H. Yoder, *The Politics of Jesus*, Grand Rapids, 1974.

77. *Op cit.*, 179–180.

78. *Op. cit.*, 180.

79. Cf. I. Baldermann, *Der Gott des Friedens und die Götter der Macht. Biblische Alternativen*, Neuenkirchen-Vluyn, 1983, 64–76.

80. R. Schnackenburg, *Alles kann, wer glaubt. Bergpredigt und Vater-unser in der Absicht Jesu*, Freiburg 1984.

81. A. Vögtle, *Was ist Friede?*, Freiburg 1983, 68 and 98.

82. H. Spaemann, "Die Stunde der Gewaltlosigkeit", in: *Geist und Leben* 57 (1984), 84.

83. J. Topel S.J., *The Way to Peace*, Maryknoll, N.Y. 1979, 139.

84. R. Pesch, "Die Überwindung der Gewalt", in: N. Lohfink/R. Pesch, *Weltgestaltung und Gewaltlosigkeit*, 73.

85. cf. J. Topel, S.J., *op. cit.*, 136.

86. A. Vögtle, *Was ist Frieden?*, 64

87. J. Topel, *op. cit.*, 141.

88. Cf. G. Labourerie, *Dieu de violence et Dieu de tendress*, Paris 1982.

89. P. Lapide, *op. cit.*, 20.

90. Cf. esp. M. L. King, *Stride Toward Freedom*, New York 1958; Id., *The Trumpet of Conscience*, New York 1968.

91. R. Pesch, *op. cit.*, 79. David Hollenbach synthesises the many voices of biblical scholars: "There can be no doubt that the New Testament proclaims a message of peace and calls those who would be Jesus' disciples to a nonviolent way of living" (*Nuclear Ethics*, New York/ Ramsey 1983, 13).

92. N. Lohfink, *Gewalt und Gewalttätigkeit im Alten Testament*, 42.

93. Cf. M. L. King, *Strength of Love*, 1963.

94. All these and many more detailed principles in M. K. Gandhi, *An Autobiography* (tr. M. Desai) Boston 1957. See also E. Erikson, *Gandhi's Truth*, New York 1969.

95. N. Lohfink, *Gewalt und Gewalttätigkeit im Alten Testament*, 199.

96. Cf. R. Girard, *op. cit.*, 224f. We find the same emphasis in Alexander Solzhenitsyn, "One Word of Truth Outweighs the World", Nobel Speech on Literature, in: *Index on Censorship* 3/4, London 1972, 26: "Violence is inevitably bound up with lie. Between them is the most intimate, most natural and fundamental link: violence can only be concealed by the lie, and the lie can be maintained only by violence".

97. R. Girard, *op. cit.*, 185f and 189.

98. I. Baldermann, *Der Gott des Friedens und die Götter der Macht*, 18.

99. K. Lange-Feldhahn, *Alternative Sicherheitskonzepte*, Tübingen 1983, 75.

100. M. Buber, *Der Jude und sein Judentum*, 1963, 642.

101. R. A. McCormick SJ, "Notes on Moral Theology", in: *Theol. Studies*, 45 (1984), 129.

102. Cf. H. Goss-Mayr, *Die Macht der Gewaltlosen*, Graz 1980, 180.

103. V. Bhave, *Gedanken*, Gladenbach 1979, N. 668.

104. R. Pesch, in: Lohfink/Pesch, *Weltgestaltung und Gewaltlosigkeit*, 67.

105. Quoted by P. Lapide, *Wie liebt man seine Frinde?*, 63.

106. R. Girard, *op. cit.*, 236.

107. R. Antonich SJ, in: H. Goss-Mayr (ed.), *Geschenk der Armen an die Reichen*, Wien 1980, 62.

108. J. W. Douglas, *The Non-Violent Cross*, London 1968, 71.

109. *Op. cit.*, 92. This is the strength of Gandhi's spirituality. He says: "The example of Jesus' suffering is a factor in the composition of my undying faith in nonviolence which rules all my actions" (Gandhi, *The Law of Love*, ed. by A. T. Hingerani, Bhvan 1962, 79).

110. H. Spaemann, "Die Stunde der Gewaltlosigkeit", in: *Geist und Leben* 57 (1984), 84.

111. *Op. cit.*, 88.

112. Gandhi quoted by P. Regamey, *Non-violence and the Christian Conscience*, London 1966, 199.

113. R. Niebuhr, *Christianity and Power Politics*, New York 1940, 10.

114. G. Strecker, *Die Bergpredigt. Ein Exegetischer Kommentar*, Gottingen 1984, 87 and 91.

115. C. F. von Weizsäcker, *Der ungesicherte Frieden*, 30.

116. V. Zsifskovits, "Gewaltlosigkeit", in: *Katholisches Soziallexikon*, 2nd ed. Innsbruck/Graz 1980, 967–978, quote 988.

117. F. Böckle, in: F. Böckle und G. Krell (eds.), *Politik und Ethik der Abschreckung. Geiträge zur Herausforderung der Nuklear-waffen*, Mainz/München 1984, 15. What my good friend Charles Curran writes on this sounds quite different: "The whole Church cannot be pacifist in our present circumstances", and "Pacifism is not necessarily a higher calling" (Analysis of the American Bishops' Pastoral Letter on Peace and War", in *Critical Concerns in Moral Theology*, Notre Dame 1984, 123–170, quotes 163 and 164). It seems that he does not see even the possibility or need to consider the option for nonviolent civilian defence as a direly needed alternative to war, while the U.S. Bishops do so explicitly. Curran apparently missed this point completely when he summarized the content of the document with these words: "A final section justifies nonviolence as choice for some individuals" (p. 125), whereas European peace researchers give much praise to this document because it does appeal explicitly to all to give proper attention to nonviolent defence as moral alternative to war. I would like to invite those who think like Curran to remember the history of slavery, when theologians and Churchmen held the opinion that "some individuals" might well set free their slaves but that the whole Church could not reject the institution of slavery. Of course, we need tolerance towards those who consider nonviolent defence a utopian "impossible possibility"; we need great understanding for politicians who would like to make this option their policy but do not find sufficient democratic support. But my conviction is that "the whole Church" should firmly and intelligently promote the cause of nonviolence, including the option for nonviolent defence. For this we must make it clear that we do not speak about a passive pacifism but rather of a most committed option for peace and justice, with all their "spiritual armour". Such an option should not be compared with a special religious vocation for some individuals. At this crossroad of human history the whole of humankind should become "pacifist" and ban any option for war.

CHAPTER FOUR

The healing power of nonviolence in all human relationships

The extreme physicalistic trend in medicine (and sometimes even in Catholic medical ethics) to limit its interest and inquiry to discrete organs made it possible to overlook the primordial importance of wholesome and healing relationships for spiritual and psychosomatic health. And no less deplorable has been the common approach to social and political problems without any thought about the healing dimension.

From both biblical and anthropological perspectives, based on a sound philosophy of personalism, social workers and healing and pastoral professionals can never overestimate the element of care for good personal and social relationships. The words about the Servant of Yahweh, "His wounds brought us healing" (Is 53:5), tell us the fundamental truths about the health and healing dimensions of nonviolence.

In the World Council of Churches there has developed, during the last decade, a wholistic understanding of both peace and healing, with particular emphasis on healthy relationships. The survey on "Health, Healing, Wholeness" brought a rich harvest of thoughts on the intimate connection between peace-reconciliation, on the one hand, and, on the other, healthful relations between man and God and between self and fellowmen. The result is the insight and purpose to foster communities which radiate health, wholeness and peace.[118]

I feel that enough attention has not yet been given to the specific healing power of a nonviolent approach in all personal relationships. This theme is still a great challenge to theology and religious pedagogy.

1. *The way to a healthy understanding of discipleship of Christ*

No doubt, there is an interplay between irrational and perverse mimesis and an inclination to destructive aggression. Superficial men ape each other in their trend to appropriation. The human ape copies the others' violence, repaying violence for violence, offence for offence. Imitation in superficial or indifferent matters reinforces the inclination to mimicry in all matters that have to do with violence, treachery and appropriation of material goods. Contamination by reciprocal fear and anguish makes things worse.

How different is the situation marked by the nonviolence of Christ! When we come to a deep trust in him, to a deeper knowledge of his healing and redeeming love, we reach a deeper knowledge of self, through him, and understand our need to be more completely healed from our violence.

It is important to see the cleansing of the temple in the context of the healing mission of Jesus. It was the fulfilment of the prophecies about the purification of Zion from unhealthy religious practices and powers (cf. Is 1:25–27; Mal 3:1–4), in intimate connection with the coming of God's kingdom in gentleness and humility. With divine authority, the Servant of Yahweh dissociates his healing mission from false cults and sacrifices, from violence and deceit, in order to make the new Zion a centre of healing and benevolent service. In the very context of the cleansing of the temple, it is said: "In the temple blind men and cripples came to him and he healed them" (Mt 21:14).[119]

Whoever is cleansed by the Servant of Yahweh from inclination to violence or its contamination can be healed from what cripples and blinds him and can come to a deep understanding of salvation and health. Cleansed from false cults and evil, we can understand better that, being called to intimate discipleship by the nonviolent Servant of Yahweh, we are called also to the cleansed and healing community of the new Zion and to solidary commitment to the gospel of peace and nonviolence. Thus we are on the road to overcoming the violence that plagues mankind.[120] In this respect, discipleship of Christ, "life in Christ Jesus", has the quality of a new creation, of new healing powers prospering in healthy and healing relationships.

2. *Finding our true identity and humanity through nonviolence*

In the light of Erik Erikson's life cycles,[121] we see how fundamental nonviolent commitment is for healthy development of psychic and spiritual health.

1) Basic trust versus mistrust

If a child consistently experiences parental love without any violence, so that he or she has no doubt about being loved and fully accepted even after a fault, that child can develop a basic trust in love. This trust does not need to be naive; it can harbour a justified distrust within healthy limits. But here, too, the first experiences with father and mother are fundamental. I agree with Erikson that later rich experiences and affirmation by nonviolent people (educators, friends, pastors, spouse, etc.) can gradually heal earlier wounds and enable the growing person to scale the walls of mistrust and find a healthy, firm trust in God, who is more kind than mother and father.

2) Autonomy versus shame and doubt

A nonviolent education of the child means also education *for* nonviolence. The child is helped to discover his or her own conscience and freedom for creative life, identity and integrity, but at the same time should come to realize that his or her autonomy and initiatives have to respect other people's conscience, autonomy and responsibility.

Nonviolent educators know how to speak to the awakening conscience of a child when violence meets the child on the level of the mimetic ape in the vicious circle of contamination, threat and deterrence. It is one of the greatest tasks in life to accept this mutuality of one's own and the other's worth. Parents inclined to violence make a great mistake in trying to break the stubborn will of their small child instead of helping him or her to understand this interaction. The "behind" of the small being's dark continent is all too frequently the seat of a painful experience, a violent invasion by those who unjustly deny the child's own will.[122] If pain, shame and doubt at this stage become a prevailing experience, the development of nonviolent freedom is greatly blocked. A healthy self-affirmation is an absolute requisite for authentic nonviolence.

3) Initiative versus guilt and aping mimesis

By its very nature, nonviolence is creative and awakens creative qualities in others. Nonviolent educators encourage the child's initiatives during this stage, although not all initiatives prove successful or fitting. Overweaning care by insecure and somehow violent educators restrict the play of initiative, thereby forcing the child to fall back into the realm of mere imitation, of conformity, of aping mimesis.

A child, who continues with the experiment of initiatives and has to live with ongoing violent disapproval, might finally appear "docile", an example of orderliness and submission, but might soon learn all kinds of "treachery". If the discovery of a child's own initiatives finally stops, there remains anguish and fear, grudge and disappointment. Later in life he or she will be afraid of unconformity and therefore may fall into the traps of mimesis, including mimicry of violence.

After such discouraging experiences in the decisive years of the life cycle, only long-lasting or very impressive experiences of genuine affirmation and encouragement for creativity and initiative can heal the wounds. Erikson tells of a healing experience of young Gandhi. The numerous taboos and prohibitions and his father's style of authority had driven the younger into rebellion, transgression of the taboos and even to small thefts. Then, struck with strong guilt feelings, he handed a written confession to his father with the request that he be given the well-earned punishment. His father, however, responded with tears of compassion. These tears purified the young man and repaired to some extent the damage. The wounds could heal.

4) Competence versus inferiority

Working to gain competence in professional and social life is important for self-worth. But false behaviour on the part of parents and educators, who make their benevolence dependent on success in school or on skill to please them, can destroy the healthy feeling of self-worth, which much never be confined to the narrow circle of "success". A nonviolent approach sees life as vocation at the service of human growth. This allows educators to help the less successful children to avoid any inferiority complex and, instead, to develop altruism, sensitivity and other precious qualities without any psychic imbalances. It belongs to the very substance of nonviolence never to destroy or damage another person's feeling of self-worth, even an opponent's. We all need, constantly, an advance of trust and affirmation.

5) Identity versus confusion

Identity supported by healthy self-worth, grounded on a convincing plan of life and respect for others in their identity and diversity, is a mark of psychic and spiritual health. It is the exact opposite of the compulsive mimesis of which René Girard has written so competently.

Wounded and wounding mimesis enters into a life's game where young people take the educator's violence into their own life's project and thus become ensnared in the mimetic reaction of repaying violence with violence and offence with offence. Identity is not really reached if the life project is psychologically framed by the determination to become, in no case, a person like father or like mother. Negation, even when justified, works for health only if the basis is a constructive project, a fundamental option as response to positive values incarnate in mature, exemplary people.

A vital fruit of healthy identity is the capacity to remain faithful to commitments made with discernment and in freedom. Such freedom-in-fidelity can mature best when nonviolence is a substantial dimension of the fundamental option. One who has gained deep insight into what nonviolence really means, and adheres to it so firmly that all his relationships are marked by it, has reached a very high and stable level of self-identity.

Young people who have rich potentialities involving considerable complexity, and who also bear in their memories conflicting experiences, may need a rather long time to resolve an otherwise creative identity crisis. Erikson has shown this, for example, in the lives of Martin Luther and Gandhi.[123]

Luther's sometimes shocking crudity was not only a kind of contamination and mimetic response to the violence of his opponents and the rude manners of his time and environment, but was due partially also to the wounds inflicted on him by a violent education. Projecting the father-image on God caused Luther terrible pain and anguish. Staupitz had a healing influence on him through his profound understanding and intuition which, at decisive points, helped Luther to regain the feeling of self-worth and thus also a secure identity. We can only ask, what would have happened if all the influential Catholic opponents of this man had shown evangelical nonviolence?

6) Intimacy versus isolation

Those who have established their own positive identity are able to sustain loyalties freely pledged, free for friendship. They have within themselves enough power to love enduringly. If one's identity is marked by commitment to nonviolence, such a person can not only keep friendships but even win opponents and enemies to a profound covenant of peace. Conflicts cannot drive nonviolent persons into bitterness and isolation. They can let people, who have different ideas and ideals, feel, "It is good to have people like you". Identity characterized by faithfulness to one's own life-project and by loyalty even to opponents is a distinctive sign of healthy humanness. Such people can rescue others from isolation and apathy by the healing power of love.

7) Creativity versus stagnation

Men and women like Gandhi and Dorothy Day are creative unto their old age. Not only are they able to transmit life in their good years and educate children well, but they transmit the highest life-values until the hour of their death. Nonviolence, in the full sense, enables them to reach out to people and to enrich them spiritually. They help others, including their opponents, to discover their own inner goodness and strength, and to make good use of them for the highest goals, such as peace. They are clearsighted in discovering effective remedies to heal public life. Refusing boredom and stagnation, they are more immune from the fascination of violence and its pseudo-ecstasies.

8) Wholeness and joy versus despair

A fulfilled existence, radiating warmth and peace, is one of the most beautiful expressions of distinctively human health and wholeness, a sign of healing "*shalom*". This integrity of the mature person throughout a life of dedication to peace, reconciliation and generous forgiveness, is a blessing for many people. "In the aging person who has taken care of things and people and has adapted himself to the trials, triumphs and disappointments of being: only in him, the fruit of the seven stages gradually ripens. I know no better word for it than integrity".[124] What the great therapist Erikson has to say here characterizes the best presuppositions for a deep understanding and practice of nonviolence, and is a harvest of all the virtues implied by nonviolence.

Hildegard Goss-Mayr, who with her husband has dedicated her whole life to the gospel of peace, reconciliation and nonviolence, knows whereof she speaks: "Let us open our eyes to see how nonviolent commitment changes people. . . . Nonviolent life and nonviolent promotion of justice help us to become truly human".[125]

People who have lived a long life in the midst of a peaceless world without being contaminated and poisoned, and have even helped others to be healed from peacelessness and violence, have, indeed, won a great victory. They have been "a light to the world". We need the warmth of these people in order to understand fully what Thomas Merton writes: "A nonviolent victory, while far more difficult to achieve, stands better chance of curing the illness instead of contracting it".[126]

One who lives on an eye-for-eye basis is blind and blinds others. Nonviolence, healing love for enemies, opens eyes which are closed to the most decisive values of humanness. This is, indeed, a great art of healing. "The capacity to understand and to love the basic truth of life belongs to the most important and, today, the absolute life-conditioning capabilities of the 'healthy person' ".[127]

Those who follow faithfully the path of biblical nonviolence care not only for their own integrity and health; they care about wholeness and salvation for all. Gandhi was convinced that a seemingly unsuccessful *satyagraha* campaign was not at all a failure if, in its course, the *satyagrahis* became stronger and better in captivity to violence and injustice — an insight which, time and again, kept up his endurance.[128]

3. *Regaining healthy and healing interpersonal relationships*

Conversion to nonviolence in personal life and social commitment means an end to mutual bedeveling, liberation from the ruinous game wherein all the participants degrade and wound both themselves and each other. Nonviolent interpersonal relationships and active participation in nonviolent action for peace and justice "are a practical form of exorcism, a *diakonia* of driving out impure devils, of attacking sin and its social damages but not the sinner. On the contrary, the sinner is taken seriously in his dignity; his capacity to learn and to renew himself is acknowledged".[129]

How can those who believe in the gospel of peace not pool their energies, today, to stop mutual bedeviling which in our age has taken the form of "deterrence" by Mutually-Assured-Destruction?

It is worthwhile to give special attention to nonviolent and healing communication. From Socrates to Plato and unto Gandhi, this aspect was considered fundamental as a sign of the strength of truthfulness and peacefulness.[130] A nonviolent messenger of peace meets friends and foes in non-assuming dialogue. He invites his opponent to share in the search for more light, for the best paths of justice and peace. There is no place for manipulation, for foul bargaining with "reinforcers" of threat and promise. Nonviolent communication speaks to conscience in full awareness of the mutuality of consciences, since the purpose is to find companions in dedication to the gospel of peace and truth. Thereby, peacefulness is an indispensable virtue that invites mutual attention and creates an atmosphere for quiet reflection.

A nonviolent servant of peace can free his or her partner or opponent from anguish and distrust. "If anguish is disappearing hatred can be disarmed, since most of the time it has its deepest roots in anguish".[131] What is good in our neighbour frequently just awaits our goodness to be activated; while lack of goodness in ourselves ensnares the other, and ourselves even more, in all our evil tendencies.

Anyone who is devoted to nonviolence will never degrade or abuse another person, since the goal is the common feast of peace in justice and truth. If, like Martin Luther King and his faithful followers, we could always truthfully assure our opponents that we would never stop loving them, despite what they might do to us, it would be a gigantic step towards mutual healing and the final victory of love and mutual respect.

Nonviolence invites genuine imitation for a genuine value-response. It can reverse the unsound and dangerous game of mimetic contamination and reaction. The poor will not enviously want to become like the rich, and the rich will appraise their insensitive greed to get richer while the poor get poorer. Those in authority and those under authority will acknowledge each other in equal dignity. The nonviolent poor will become more assured by the strength of truth. Both rich and poor will become free for the abiding values and goods. They will help each other to understand the sickening mechanism that calls for violence in order to keep what is acquired through injustice and/or violence. In shared search for justice and peace, they will entrust themselves to the protection of truth and solidarity. Healed from the greed for still more material goods, they will become free for each other, for enrichment by truth and peace.

4. *Towards peace with God's creation*

From the beginning, God entrusted the earth to man. "The Lord God took man and put him in the Garden of Eden to till it and care for it" (Gen 2:15). Creation's beauty invites humankind to praise God and to rejoice in him. The wealth of God's gifts invites us to solidarity as the one family of the creator. After having saved all species of animals as well as man, God includes the animals in his covenant with Noah. Man should care for them, but they also should nourish him. "Every creature that lives and moves shall be food for you; I give you them all, as once I gave you all the green plants" (Gen 9:3).

Man must not treat animals violently, nor is he allowed a destructive stewardship. "This is the sign of the covenant which I establish with you and with your descendants after you, and with every living creature that is with you, all birds and cattle, all the wild animals with you on earth" (Gen 9:8–10). God teaches man to take all creatures into the praise of his creator, not only by words but by the whole way he exercises his stewardship and treats animals and plants.

Therapeutic conversion to nonviolence can heal one of the dangerous diseases of our culture: the destructive turn to poisoning things — drugs, nicotine, alcohol, etc. — and, in the context of exploitation, the ecological environment. The materialistic growth-mania for more and more production and more and more markets for selling unnecessary and even damaging products is a sin against the generations to come. What shall we leave to them: rubbish, atomic weapons numerous enough to make the earth uninhabitable, a poisoned atmosphere, polluted water?

Groups of alert citizens in favour of ecological responsibility can, by solidary nonviolent initiatives, produce a number of therapeutic results. They form an ecological conscience, they take responsibility into their own hands instead of delegating it to a slothful bureaucracy, they are learning how to handle conflicts in a peaceful way before these become explosive. Well prepared and conducted initiatives for ecological purposes can be a meaningful exercise for a future civilian nonviolent defence, which is unthinkable without the careful use and preservation of the earth's unrenewable resources.

Our vocation to peace with God's creation should be greatly alarmed when we hear about plans to carry armaments and war even into the stratosphere, with unimaginable risks for the whole planet. Let, instead, the artificial satellites discover the wounds we have already inflicted on our spaceship Earth, in order to find the appropriate remedies!

5. *From a success-oriented ethics towards an ethics of responsibility*

Incurable capitalism (including state capitalism which apes the capitalism of private owners) has one of its roots in the Calvinistic doctrine of predestination, and, looking for the much desired sign of being among the predestined, chose to find it in material, economic and political success. These "predestined people" (in their own wild imagination) can then look down on the downtrodden and poor as inferior, rejected people. This whole ideology tends to a peaceless division of humankind into successful people, who praise themselves as "God's chosen race", and the miserable and exploited ones on whom the wealthy inflict the blame of being abandoned by God.

At the beginning, this ideology gave criteria about an honest way of achieving success, but in the course of success and secularization all barriers to greed and growth-mania fell down. I had ample opportunity to observe in South Africa the praxis of this ideology. At times we can observe on TV the rage with which white policemen beat black people who are not willing to accept their sad role. We can only wonder about such hardened consciences, and wonder how people who believe in Christ, the Redeemer of all, can cling to their "success" by subjecting others to a state of slavery.

However, we should not just look for an alibi by gazing at the Republic of South Africa with its apartheid. Are we not all somehow indoctrinated by a success-oriented education in public schools, and even by a success-oriented ethics which puts trust in the armament race and the system of "successful deterrence"? Let us take a close look at the tensions between the extremely affluent industrial nations and the extremely poor "developing countries", whose very breath is taken away by wealthy nations. The usury of cruelly high interest rates is, indeed, a violent means of keeping poor nations in intolerable debt.

Dealing with pseudo-innocence and self-righteousness as a source of violence and lust for power, psychotherapist Rollo May calls for a serious examination of conscience and a new, healing awareness: "In America, pseudo-innocence has a history as long as the country's. A 'chosen people' set sail from England, turning its back on a Europe that, for it, stood for sin. . . . What about the religious persecution that soon sprang up even in the 'New England'? What about the beginning genocide of the Indians . . . Franklin shows how the citizens identify the design of Providence, the will of God, with their own and their countrymen's self-interest. . . . This is the hallmark of pseudo-innocence: always identify your self-interest with the design of Providence".[132]

The mimetic race for success, coupled with all shades of pseudo-innocence and self-righteousness, has destroyed millions of families or, at least, impoverished family relationships. At the global level it is one of the main roots of international conflicts and wars. A prevalent striving for success, especially if it is, consciously or unconsciously, connected with an individual or collective complex of "chosen-ness" above others, makes people hard-hearted and impatient about higher values and the real needs of their neighbour and of other nations.

There is no way to peace and a nonviolent culture without uncovering such a pathological background and without commitment to profound conversion and patient work for a new public consciousness.

For these and many other reasons, self-education for nonviolence and an all-encompassing change of education in Church and society, with high priority for nonviolence, becomes vital in view of the explosive situation that threatens all of us. This awesome task requires firmness and patience (*patientia:* an ancient name for nonviolence. Thomas Aquinas called it "the bravest part of fortitude"). All this should flow together in an ethics of responsibility, understood particularly as an ethics of committed response to the gift and task of peace, and response to redemption for salvation, wholeness and nonviolence.

Constructive love of neighbour, understood as the virtue and art of turning our enemies into friends, requires long-suffering patience especially in the social, political and international fields: a task which is not even thinkable for a short-lived success ethics.

An ethics of ongoing conversion (part of an ethics of responsibility) needs a synthesis of lofty goals and the art of finding the next possible step, the best possible open-ended compromise or strategy which, unfortunately, cannot always embody the fullness of the Sermon on the Mount. But strategies, if they are to lead to peace, must be coherent. Each step must be in the right direction and made peaceably.

Our violent world, geared totally for success, power and wealth, is obsessed by the makeable. To the degree that interest is concentrated on the makeable, on quick success, there ensues a certain disregard for the fullness of life and for our vocation "to bear fruit in love", as the Bible teaches us. Nonviolence, in its full meaning, aims at the growth of the reign of love and peace. And this is infinitely more important "for the life of the world" than any external success.

For us Christians conversion from external success to "bearing fruit in love, peace and justice" is possible and is the only saving road in view of our faith in the cross and resurrection of Christ. A distinctively Christian ethics of responsibility cares, above all, for the quality of our faith, which alone can enable us to bear fruits in healing and redeeming love. Herein lies the test of our trust in God, who can and will raise the dead to the fullness of life.

All this radically contradicts man-made religions, with their justification of violence and even of "holy" wars. It contradicts the seeming virtues of those who consider themselves to be the ones "blessed by success" over the poor and oppressed. Commitment to the gospel of peace and nonviolence needs virtues other than those of violent warriors and success-oriented people. To take up the cause of the kingdom of peace, to fight in union with the Prince of Peace, "calls for all the strength, courage, endurance, risk taking, brains, guts, sweat and blood that any other war requires. The case is simply that these things are applied differently: to taking up a cross, following in the footsteps of the Servant-Messiah, losing one's life in order to gain it".[133]

The apparent quick successes of violence reinforce the spiral of new follow-ups of violence and the mechanisms which deprive people of true freedom for higher good and values. "On the other hand, reconciliation, forgiveness and nonviolence break up the determinisms of insensitive power. Human relationships are restored. Those who forgive gain a new freedom for a new kind of relationship".[134] This leads us again to the central relevance of healthy and healing interrelations.

6. *No other way of healing our society from criminality*

The superpowers' system of deterrence has its mirror image in our ever growing and ever more diversified criminality. There is seldom a year in which the rate of increase in crime is less than the increase in gross national production. Besides, the criminal system in which criminals have to atone for their misdeeds — if they are not wealthy enough to be "absolved" — is frequently, in fact, a masters' school of skilled criminality where, in horrifying relationships, the worst inmates teach the beginners.

It is high time for our success-oriented and violent-impatient society to show the courage to make a thoroughgoing diagnosis of this situation and its deepest roots. Those roots can be found in the "still acceptable" (?) system of the superpowers' mutual deterrence, in the widespread violence shown in the mass media for people's entertainment, in the materialistic striving for success, in the recklessness of competition, and in a success-oriented "value free" (value ignoring) educational system, with an unbelievable neglect of education for wisdom, patience, peace and nonviolence.

Our unsuccessful correctional system is only one of the warnings in the midst of a multitude of events and situations that call for peace-education, including education in nonviolence. This is surely one of the things most needed in our "wealth" societies and, indeed, all over the world. We have to recognize and acknowledge the escapism into vindictive "justice" which seeks scapegoats especially among the outcasts, the unskilled and unsuccessful.

What is called for is a total conversion and a solidary commitment to healing our ailing culture.

NOTES

118. Cf. P. Potter, "Healing and Salvation", in: *The Ecumenical Review* 33 (1981), 333; P. Potter, "A House of Living Stones", in: *The Ecumenical Review* 35 (1983), 350–364.

119. This question is well treated by V. Eller, *War and Peace*, 130ff. In the context of healing, the cleansing appears not as a violent act, as some thought. But with Eller I would insist that the cleansing of Zion is Christ's privilege and duty, not to be imitated by those of "lesser authority".

In his challenging book, *Christians and Nonviolence in the Nuclear Age*, Mystic 1982, 45f, G. A. Vanderhaar applies the cleansing of the temple to the "idolatry" and the boasting given to nuclear armament. He comes to the conclusion: "The temple today, that area of life in which one's ultimate concern is exercised, ought to be a place of healing, not hurting, of zeal for the ways of the Lord, not the pursuit of power and pride and profit".

120. Cf. R. Pesch, "Neues Testament und die Überwindung der Gewalt", in: N. Lohfink / R. Pesch, *Weltgestaltung und Gewaltlosigkeit*, 76f.

121. Cf. E. Erikson, *Insight and Responsibility*, New York 1964; *Identity and Crises*, New York 1968; *Gandhi's Trust*, New York 1969; *Young Man Luther*, New York 1958; cf. B. Häring, *Free and Faithful in Christ*, vol. I, St Paul Publications, Slough 1978, 168–181.

122. Erikson gives great attention to this point in young Luther's experience. R. May (*op. cit.*, 23) is also outspoken on this phenomenon, which points beyond individual experience: "Violence has its breeding ground in impotence and apathy. . . . If we make people powerless, we promote their violence rather than its control".

123. Cf. *Young Man Luther*, 242: "In Luther a partially unsuccessful and fragmentary solution of the identity crisis of youth aggravated the crisis of manhood".

124. E. Erikson, *Insight and Responsibility*, 128.

125. H. Goss-Mayr, *Der Mensch vor dem Unrecht*, Wien 1976, 76.

126. T. Merton, *Faith and Violence, Christian Teaching and Christian Practice*, Notre Dame 1976, 12.

127. C. F. von Weizsäcker, *Friedlosigkeit als seelische Krankheit*, 50.

128. See Gandhi's autobiography.

129. H. E. Bahr, *Versöhnung und Widerstand*, 129.

130. Cf. W. Kremp, *Gewaltlosigkeit und Wahrheit. Studien zur Therapie der Gewalt bei Pdaton und Gandhi*, Meisenheim 1975.

131. P. Lapide, *op. cit.*, 37.

132. R. May, *op. cit.*, 50ff.

133. V. Eller, *War and Peace*, 152.

134. R. Antonich, in: H. Goss-Mayr (ed.), *Geschenk der Armen an die Reichen*, 40.

CHAPTER FIVE

The healing power of nonviolence in the realm of politics

It is a worldwide growing conviction that, in our day, the option between violence and nonviolence is an option between the extreme danger of extinction and the chance of a dignifying survival.

Today, we commit ourselves to liberation from socially unacceptable life conditions, from exploitation and oppression; we do not renounce our democratic freedom and our freedom of conscience under the threat of inhumane totalitarian systems; we do not intend to fight violently even to the point of mutual extinction. The only meaningful and promising way is militant nonviolence as practised by Gandhi and Martin Luther King.

During the past sixteen hundred years the theory of "just war" intended to keep war and warfare within narrow limits whenever there was no chance of avoiding it. There was a strong emphasis on the proportionality between hoped-for benefits and damage, and on the exemption of non-combatant civil populations. Under the present military situation these conditions cannot and will never be observed. Taking as basis the best Christian tradition on "just war", we come to the same conclusion as that of another Christian tradition: the tradition of pacifism.

Pacifism, however, does not mean renunciation of self-defence in such situations as our tradition considered self-defence obligatory. The Catholic Bishops of East Germany have come to the conclusion expressed in an emphatic question: "Under these conditions, does not the frequently disregarded ideal of nonviolence, as proclaimed by Jesus in the Sermon on the Mount, win an undreamed-of rational affirmation?"[135]

The Bishops of West Germany are supported by the almost unanimous consensus of biblical scholars when they protest against an individualistic narrowing of the meaning of God's message, and particularly of the biblical doctrine on nonviolence. "From the spirit of the Sermon on the Mount, conclusions are to be drawn also for politics. But how is this to be done? Which conclusions are to be drawn? The question is how the commands of Jesus are to be applied to the political realm".[136]

In response to the question, the Bishops emphasize, above all, the healing power of redeemed and redeeming, nonviolent love: "This love will try with the utmost energy and perseverance to win the opponents for peace, to offer nonviolent solutions of conflicts, and fields of cooperation. Thus the devilish circle of violence must be broken; aggression and confrontation must be dismantled".[137]

For a long period in the Old Testament salvation of the individual was considered much less than the saving plan and healing love of God for his chosen people and humanity as a whole. During the Babylonian exile and with the growth of faith in the resurrection, individual responsibility and God's care for everyone came more to the fore. John Topel synthesises the first chapters of the Book of Wisdom: "God revealed his law and raised kings to heal human society as a whole, which as a whole has been afflicted with the contagion of sin (Wis 1:4)".[138]

Christ's preaching on the coming kingdom of God is not less all-embracing. The emphasis on conversion of the heart is not an invitation to a narrow heart. The kingdom of God intends to heal and to save the whole of humankind by the pacifying power of his love and nonviolence.

The preceding chapters elaborated more on healing within the realm of interpersonal relationships, and from there, of the social life. But it would be unrealistic to dream that good interpersonal relationships automatically change social conditions. These must be given direct attention, just as the kingdom of God directly includes the various forms in which redeemed solidarity is or should be expressed. Ingo Baldermann points to the woeful experiences in Hitler's time: "Men who were peaceful family fathers or good sons at once had nothing else in mind than to kill the sons and fathers of families on the other side and even, 'when it had to be done', to kill women and children".[139]

It cannot be stressed enough that the biblical message of peace is all-embracing: peace with God, inner peacefulness, peace in family and neighbourhood, peace in Church and society, peace among nations. Not less universal is the dynamic of peace: nonviolence. It is a healing power not only for the individuals but also for society, for social and economic relations and structures, and for politics in all its dimensions. To disregard this remedy has catastrophic consequences for all.

1. *A healing power on the way to a healthier society*

We have to fight constantly against the "sin of the world", which embodies itself in institutions, processes, structures, social conflicts, and in a confused public opinion. All this tends to reinforce itself by contamination and mutual reaction. No society is simply healthy. If a nation wants to play a peaceful and peacemaking role in the concert of nations, then this very intention compels it to give even greater attention to fostering inner peace and justice. Festering wounds in a country's social life have poisoning effects on international relations. Violent oppression of citizens, abuse of minorities and violent revolutions increase the potential of violence and treachery. The production of images of "devilish enemies" within a nation favour an even worse production of enemy-images in international politics. Today's world is full of examples.

In my work, *Free and Faithful in Christ*, I have treated social ethics in the perspective of healing as well as of liberation. It is the enormous task of healing public life, whereby everything is directed towards the healing power of the gospel of peace and nonviolence. But much more effort in this direction is necessary. I am in full sympathy with the Latin American project of a theology of liberation, especially with those who give high priority to nonviolence.[140] And I am convinced that many preoccupations shown by the Church authorities would be more easily dissipated if this theology of liberation had already fully integrated the perspective of healing nonviolence in its whole approach.

Another worry is the use of Marxist analysis in part of liberation theology. In my opinion we can and should distinguish between the many parts of the analysis offered by Marx himself, which have proven false, and others which were concrete observations made in Marx's time and which in a similar way can still be observed today. But one thing seems evident: Karl Marx does not know the healing power of nonviolence; it simply has no place in his explanation of the necessary process of social conflicts. A liberation theology which gives the appropriate place to healing love and reconciliation can hardly be suspected of being ensnared in Marxist ideology as such.

It is absurd to harbour suspicion of Marxist ideology only because one calls for social justice and renewal of society while clearly advocating nonviolence just as the prophets of old did. Marx's fault is not that he observed the fact that oppression and violence by the powerful might provoke violence by the oppressed. His disastrous error is to consider violence as a necessary law of history and — this is the summit of his ideology — as a law of progress or of promoting progress, if the oppressed become able to use greater violence than the oppressors. In other words, Karl Marx observes, from within, the circle of violence-for-violence's sake, affirming this as a necessary and proven law of scientific socialism.

Marx's error is not that he protests against religion being used in favour of the oppressors, but that he affirms that religion does this necessarily. To my knowledge, all Latin American liberation theology is on the side of the prophetic denunciation of such abuse and believes that true religion — Christian faith — radically opposes any selfish use of religion.

Marx analyses socio-economic structures, relationships and processes from within the circle of violence. He rejects any kind of ethical-prophetic socialism or any social reformer who believes that renewal can and must be done by breaking this deadly circle.

On this point I met calculated confusion during my stay in Brazil. When men, like Helder Camara, make the strongest possible appeal to everyone to get out of the vicious circle and solve problems in nonviolent ways, but then add a warning to the powerful perpetrators of violence to the effect that "either you accept the appeal to nonviolent solution in favour of justice or you increase the danger of violent reactions" — for this, he is called "Marxist" by the confusionists.

Being Christians and believers in redemption does not at all blind us to the *fact* that violence and treachery have a contaminating effect: that oppression, by itself, "calls for" violence, although we, as Christians, beg all to get out of the vicious circle by conversion to justice, peace and nonviolence. Our distinctive and decisive faith is that, because of redemption and in the strength of faith, we can climb out of the devilish pattern of violence, exploitation and oppression.

The exploiters and the powerful, who believe in violence in order to prevent social justice, are much closer to Marxism than they imagine. They reject redemption from sin, oppression, violence, just as much as Marxists do. The difference is only that they do it in favour of the advantageous "established order" (of deplorable inequality) while Marxists "believe" in violence to overthrow that order. Both — although in opposite positions — refuse redemption, peace and justice.

We cannot deny that, in past history, even churchmen believed so much in a certain interpretation of "original sin" that they suspected everywhere a sinful use of liberty among the poor and the oppressed, while attributing wisdom and full redemption to themselves and to those on the throne. Therefore, they blocked genuine social and political reforms.

Under a Marxist regime this kind of trend is probably even worse. Do powerful Marxist regimes believe that the people themselves can probe the truth about society? If so, why are they so suspicious, and why do they use violence to impose the "orthodox interpretation" of Marxism? The disregard for the common people who think differently is striking. Real Marxism, as we experienced it during this century, is also marked by an arrogant impatience which impels its supporters, time and again, to use violence, war, revolution, concentration camps, terrorism and brain-washing to hasten their goals.

With all this said, the other side of the coin can and must now be brought to light. Why should we deny that, among people who have been raised as Marxists, there are many who search for truth? Redemption can operate among them too; while also among Christians there are many who sinfully resist the promptings of redemption. It is a prime duty to unmask the hidden atheist in ourselves, the hidden ideologist contaminated by violence. Only then can we try to exercise the Socratic "midwifery" to help those on the oher side to discover the good, the hunger and thirst for truth and justice, in themselves. There is no other way to promote peace and reconciliation and to give witness to redemption from violence.

The assurance that we would like to walk the path of nonviolence and nonviolent renewal of society, *if* the other side would co-operate and walk with us, is an unacceptable excuse. Nonviolence, love of enemy, must be creative, initiative, inspired by the power of redemption. If we acquire the spirituality of nonviolence and meet the other side with genuine love, giving them an advance of trust about their good will (which can grow) while we probe all the ways of nonviolent solutions, then we can trust in the help of God.

This is true also in our approach to wealthy and powerful "capitalists". We have no right to declare them "hopeless cases". Nonviolence based on faith never stops practising and proclaiming the gospel of peace and reconciliation. It will give the other side an advance of trust in view of the tremendous, undeserved, advance God gives us by his healing grace.

Nonviolence practises a constructive, creative dialogue. Our opponent should have the good feeling that we realize we need him, his experience, his vision in order to probe together for fuller truth and to find, time and again, the next possible step in the right direction.

On the road towards peace there is need for open-ended compromises. Such compromises in no way imply betrayal of the goals and ideals. Rather, the compromise acknowledges that both sides are pilgrims and can only make a step at a time in the shared endeavour for reconciliation and peace in justice. All concerned must realize that the healing of public life, as well as total conversion of persons, are long processes wherein all need patience with themselves and with those who think differently.

Nonviolent promoters of ecological healing and of nonviolent defence, as alternative to the present system, will respect the democratic procedure of patient work to gain public interest and genuine conviction. Nonviolent minorities in a democracy cannot ask for more than the right and opportunity to work so that minorities will one day become the majority. This will succeed best if opponents are not bedeviled, not accused of ill will. Otherwise any talk of nonviolence will be neither convincing nor credible.

The more respectfully the dialogue between the parties is conducted, the healthier will be the democracies and the more effective their nonviolent civilian defence. This is true also of the social classes. A democracy in which the governing party is not willing to recognize good proposals from the opposition parties, and where those in opposition criticize the government without attention to truth and fairness, is not yet mature enough for the alternative of civilian defence.

In a society where nonviolence and mutual respect have high priority, neither employers' associations nor trade unions will ask themselves first whether they have enough power and money to win a round in a conflict, but, rather, will look together for what is right and economically feasible, for what best serves the common good. This kind of thinking will mark not only their public declarations but also their reflections behind locked doors.

In a nonviolent society, pressure groups will be more easily unmasked and checked, and can be finally convinced that unjust pressure degrades them as well as those whom they seek to influence. On principle, a nonviolent society will give attention first to socially weaker groups and minorities. In such a society everyone will become better able to see what kind of behaviour is still ensnared in the vicious circle of bigotry, greed and violence, and is in need of change.

In a nonviolent society, great energies will be released for the promotion of a creative culture wherein all can make their contribution in reconciled diversity.

2. *Liberation from the slavery of war: Wars have no right to exist*

a) *Peace is possible*

That peace is possible and that, consequently, humankind can rid itself of the age-old slavery of war is the constantly repeated message of recent popes, from John XXIII to John Paul II. This message and appeal come from the very faith in redemption of humankind. The test of a peace-movement is faith in the redemption from the sin of violence. It is the foundation of peacefulness and the peace-mission of believers.[141] Where this faith is strong, it will be easier to dissipate the utopian dream that peace can be preserved through increase of armament and mutual threat of annihilation.

Much credit should go to René Girard for having proposed the question about nonviolence as central aspect of redemption through Jesus Christ, the nonviolent Servant, and without the slightest insinuation that this would diminish the redemption for life everlasting. Furthermore, he has exposed man's temptation to "create" his god in the image and likeness of violent man, of man's vindictive justice. Christ has shown us the full image of God: "He who sees me sees the Father"; and thus commands us to "Be compassionate as your heavenly Father". Redemption can no longer be treated without particular attention to the therapeutic and liberating power of nonviolence, as embodied and revealed by Christ.

If some forms of liberation theology meet objections because their vision is one-sided and incomplete, one should also become aware of various other one-sided theological approaches. Think, for instance, of the theories on the redemptive sacrifice of Christ which pay no attention to Jesus' nonviolence in fulfilment of his redemptive mission and at the same time emphasise vindictive justice as foundation of theories on New Testament sacrifice. Especially in view of the signs of the times, this was and is a dangerous narrowing of the Testament.

Jesus' entry into Jerusalem before his passion and crucifixion — humble and meek, on a donkey — and his cleansing of the temple in the context of healing — all in preparation for the full meaning of his death — are in clear fulfilment of one of the great peace promises of the Old Testament prophets, a sign of the coming of the kingdom of peace and nonviolence. "Rejoice, rejoice, daughter of Zion, for, see, your king is coming to you, his cause won, his victory gained, humble and mounted on an ass, the young of a she-ass. He shall banish chariots from Ephraim and war horses from Jerusalem; the warriors' bow shall be banished. He shall speak peaceably to every nation" (Zech 9:9–10).

The motive of atonement will not be devalued, but purified and immensely enriched, purged of ideas from man-made religions which projected their own violence onto the image of God. Under human violence, Christ has suffered the most atrocious embodiment of the "sin of the world". He really atones for man's violence and treachery. He dies as revealer of the liberating and healing truth, and bears the full burden of sinful mankind. By his very nonviolence he fully restores the honour of the Father, revealing the Father's true image. He dies for those who crucify him, for all of us sinners. And by his healing love he breaks up the circle of enmity, violence and vindictiveness, and shows us the way to a healing peace in justice.

The Father's honour has surely not required his Son's cruel suffering, as such, to be offered for any reason of vindictive justice. He is in no way accountable for the wickedness suffered by his Son. Cruelty is not wanted by the Father or the Son. The responsibility is ours, each time we sin, especially if we sin by any kind of violence against any one of Christ's brothers and sisters.

Those who suffer in the same way as Christ did, nonviolently, and who are also motivated by hunger and thirst for healing justice, share in his redemptive work. They atone, giving honour to the Father by manifesting his true image.

Refusal of the way of nonviolence in the process of healing and of love of enemy is an existential heresy of the worst kind, especially in view of the signs of the present time, when the alternative of non-violent conflict-solving becomes a question of "to be or not to be" for humankind. It is not possible to speak of Christ's sacrifice while ignoring the role of nonviolence.[142]

Especially in view of the eruptive signs of the times, the fundamental option of faith in Jesus Christ requires faith in redemption from violence, and the firm purpose to co-operate with the Redeemer so that people may come to believe that "Peace is Possible". Such fundamental option has a healing power for the "life of the world".

b) *The time has come to set us free from war*

Two thousand years after the coming of Christ, the Redeemer, who has wrought peace and reconciliation and shown us the way of nonviolent love and commitment to justice, there should not be any more wars. The fact that there are wars and, worse still, the threat of mutual annihilation, creates a tremendous challenge for all who call themselves Christian. It has now become a question of "healing from folly".[143]

It is part of the strength of the pastoral letter of the U.S. Bishops on "The Challenge of Peace" that it gives proper attention, with careful argumentation, to the two streams of Christian tradition: fundamental option for radical nonviolence and the theory on "just war". The U.S. Bishops come to the conclusion that in view of the atrocity of the so-called traditional weapons and the real danger in any major war of degenerating into an uncontrollable nuclear defeat of all humanity, war is no longer to be considered a morally acceptable way of self-defence. There is no longer any semblance of proportionality between the evil to be feared and the good that might result. The logic is such that many episcopates now are appealing for greater consideration of nonviolence as the morally viable way of self-defence.

It is my firm conviction that human history and insight into the full meaning of redemption have come to the point that only a nonviolent, well-prepared and spiritually-grounded civilian defence is the only alternative left. But, indeed, this is far more than a lamentable "only", for it would be a qualitative leap in human development to decide for this alternative.

c) *Let us begin to do whatever can be done to make this possible*

A realistic observer of the present sad situation of humankind — who is also a man of faith — tells us: "If I did not believe in God's peace, the peace of the future would be for me no more than a shadow on the abyss".[144] Von Weizsäcker reminds us that changes similar to liberation from war have happened in the course of history: for instance, the victory over the deeply rooted and strongly ideologized system of slavery, which once brought similar advantages to the privileged class, just as war does to the military-industrial complex today.

Many have tried to prove that a peaceful humanity is not possible because of an inherited instinct for aggression. But did not many people prove by their whole life that the precious energies dissipated in aggression can be channelled for great causes, including the cause of peace? It is a question of motivation and firm convictions. With many researchers, I hold that instincts are much less dangerous than ideologies. If we want a nonviolent culture, we have to overcome all ideologies that have glorified violence or defined it as a fate to be accepted. Thomas Merton agrees with Simone Weil that "the acceptance of war as an unavoidable fatality is the root of the power of politicians' ruthless and obsessive commitment to violence".[145]

As Christians who believe in redemption through Jesus, who is Nonviolence Incarnate, we have an inalienable vocation to overcome these ideologies by the strength of our faith and by our witness, but also with good reasoning, which should be possible for the redeemed.

d) *Liberation from bedeviling images of foes*

Peace researchers have pointed to the fact that, throughout history, bellicose leaders and classes have constructed totally deformed images of foes, which made them look like incarnate devils. They needed this for self-justification and for instigating their subjects and soldiers to atrocious warfare. The "spook", spreading fearful images of the foes, played a major role in all the terrible wars of this century. It was practised to the point where the nationalistic war or wars, which were fought mainly for hegemonic and economic reasons, looked like "holy" wars. As a result, crimes that cried to heaven could be commanded and obediently fulfilled with a terribly "good conscience".

Rollo May has given sharp attention to this pathological trend. The deeply rooted foe-image prevents any serious effort to appreciate the adversary's motives, fears and anguish. "Nations, in their misreading of the motives of other nations, can do what the paranoid patient does: they work against their own interests because of their projection of hostility and aggression". Dr May thinks this was the case with the United States when the Russian hawks deposed Krushchev and installed a less friendly government. If smouldering suspicions then break into flame, the vicious circle is complete and all are trapped in the holocaust. "At the outset of every war we hastily transform our enemy into the image of the demoniac, and then, since it is the devil we are fighting, we can shift into a war without asking ourselves all the troublesome psychological and spiritual questions that war arouses".

Time and again, analysing pseudo-innocence, May challenges his co-citizens: "Lacking the sense of our complicity, most Americans also lack the element of mercy, which may well turn out to be a *sine qua non* of living in this world with an attitude of humanity".[146]

However, I would not dare to say "most Americans". During the Vietnam war I had an experience in contrast. Waiting at Tokyo airport for my flight, I was joined by an American soldier, a Protestant, who lacked neither the "sense of complicity" nor the "element of mercy" or compassion, as he spoke of the atrocities ordered in war. He told me of his firm purpose not to go back to Vietnam. Immediately after this talk another American greeted me, emphasising his identity as Catholic. With an evident sense of pride, he told me that so many years ago he was "up there" in the sky, dropping bombs on the city. To my question about how he could ever participate in killing civilian people, he responded angrily, "People? Nonsense. Japanese!" Even after all the years, he could not see the Japanese as "people", as "persons".

Everything possible must be done to inoculate public opinion against this dangerous virus, this dementia. (Webster's Third International Dictionary defines dementia as "madness", and gives as example, "the *dementia* of national hatreds".) In these manoeuvres we meet again the inevitable connection between violence and treachery, lies and manipulation. "Persecution mania on both sides, in which we are deeply ensnared, is the great foe before us and in us. . . . Since this is the enemy of all men, should not those who, up to now, looked on each other only as foes feel obliged to make a covenant for a joint fight against this foe?" [147] In this effort each partner has to begin with an exorcism to free itself from attitudes which play in the devil's game.

For the West (the NATO countries) the first thing to do is to give all the nations under communist regime absolute assurance that they never will use nuclear weapons against them. No longer should politicians be heard speaking words to the effect that the West cannot exempt people of other nations from being hostages in case of war. Absolute assurance must be given that non-combatants will never again be treated as they were during the Second World War.

There must be official and unambiguous regrets for this kind of action and mentality. The arbitrary destruction of the entire population of Nagasaki and Hiroshima would, by itself, be compelling reason for a national day of atonement and expression of repentance. German politicians should be extremely sensitive about the wounds inflicted on the spirit of nations and populations under Hitler's atrocities. If we want — and we must want — to help the other side to rid itself of the spook of devil-images about the West, we must humbly remember our past. Moreover, it is realistic to note the problem that totalitarian regimes "need" the bedeviling foe-images in order to keep themselves in power and to make their nations ready for the armament race. Is that what we want? [148]

First, we must reach out to world opinion and to the nations which we have frightened with past actions and/or with bullying expressions of nuclear threat. But we must be equally concerned to help the governments and parties whose system we fear as threat to our liberty, in order to rid them of the exaggerated image of the West as being bellicose and lusting for domination. This needs a new way of thinking and many deeds as credible signs of a turn to nonviolent attitudes: small steps that will earn a well-deserved trust about our peacefulness.

Within the present system of Mutually Assured Destruction (MA.D.), there is no exorcism strong enough to drive out the spook of devil-images of the foe. "The system of deterrence needs the foe for self-assertion. But we are enabled to know that we need the other as our neighbour and that he needs us".[149] On the basis of nonviolent thinking and the fostering of a nonviolent culture and politics, this plain acknowledgement is the way to free ourselves and the other side from the trap of the system of deterrence, which keeps alive the vicious circle of fear and anguish, and thereby produces the devilish foe-images unto an eventually inescapable war.

e) *On the road to "interior politics" within the one human family*

The nation-states of past centuries, which fought each other in atrocious wars, considered their sovereignty, above all, as the right to declare and to conduct wars. The Christian faith in God, as the one Father of the one human family under his sovereignty, had little impact. Yet, there is no chance for liberation from the savage slavery of war without radical conversion in this fundamental question of faith. This is, indeed, a central theme of the peace mission undertaken by the popes and the universal Church.

The increasing experience of the whole of humankind living on the one spaceship, Earth, and our faith in the one God and Father call us to a new approach to politics. We have to work for a peace order established and promoted by some kind of "worldwide interior politics as the only viable alternative to the present block-politics".[150] The planning should not envision or move towards a powerful superstate. Rather, it has to be worked out in the patient construction of international organs for the protection of peace and justice and for courts of arbitration, with full respect for the principle of subsidiarity (federal united nations).

The road is long and full of obstacles. The goal cannot be reached completely without a worldwide conversion to the spirituality and practice of nonviolence. But this does not dispense us from structural efforts for a peace order to be accepted by all nations. In the meantime, the effort must at least make the nation-states, great powers and superpowers realize that their power politics is an extremely dangerous, pathological aberration which cries for healing.

f) *Shared endeavour to get out of the "deterrence" trap*

The present state of mutual deterrence, with weaponry that could destroy all humankind ten times over and make the earth uninhabitable for ever, is the most extreme form of human pathology on all sides. The Second Vatican Council (cf. *Gaudium et Spes*, 81) speaks forcefully of "an utterly treacherous trap for humankind". How is such unreasonableness to be healed?

First, all must confess their part of responsibility and guilt. Secondly, all must realize and acknowledge that they need each other (must work together) to disentangle this untenable situation. But all this will not really work until a strong worldwide opinion calls for conversion and for structural changes in the direction of nonviolence. Meanwhile, the small steps now possible must be taken to come to a less pathological order and gradually to healthy communication and mutual good will.

Public opinion should severely censure all kinds of boasting with great parades of military might, or even of superiority, and all violent speeches and violent reactions to them.

In the indispensable task of unmasking injustice, oppression and treachery, all generalizations must be avoided, especially if they could hurt other nations or other social classes. For instance, if we disapprove a practice of the leaders of a Communist party or the government of Russia, we should never say, "the Russians", laying blame on a whole population. Every nation has its saints, its innocents and its "devils", including our own nation, and probably in about the same proportion.

Efforts to overcome enmity and distrust are not to be confused with either an ostrich policy or a defeatist resignation in view of the heavy heritage which the other side has to digest and to overcome. Rather, let us always deal first with our own aggravating heritage and our readiness to deal with it. Only if we ascribe to the other side the goodwill and the ability to free itself consciously from the bad heritage can we hope to find in ourselves the motive and capability to do the same.

As a typical example I think of Lenin's "classical" comments on the bellicose character of Marxist socialism. "Wars of socialism, once victorious in one country against bourgeois and reactionary countries, must not be excluded".[151] "Socialists cannot be against all war without ceasing to be socialists; they can never be against revolutionary wars".[152] Particularly striking are some of Lenin's words on using pacifists as useful idiots, while being at the same time full of contempt for any kind of pacifism. He writes angrily to a Communist who seemed to exclude such dishonest manoeuvres "But by whom, when and where was it ever denied that the Communist party should make use of this when the goal is to destroy the enemy, the bourgeoisie?"[153]

Those in the West who intend to join peace movements organized and guided by Communist parties following Moscow's directives should be at least alert to this kind of socialist "orthodoxy". It cannot easily be denied that the style of leadership and party-control makes it difficult to overcome such "dogmas". But it must also be seen that much has happened since Lenin, and in view of the new, very precarious situations, we should credit the Soviet leaders with an ability to overcome the shades of their past. This is especially credible if the West contributes its share to create a new spirit and style in international politics.

But the first thing necessary is that political leaders in the West should clean up their own house. They should well remember that their predecessors — or even the present generation of Western politicians — in their oral and written commentaries have done not much better or have, themselves, committed sins of the same kind. Suffice it, here, to remember the "dogma" of U.S. leaders in the Second World War of "unconditional surrender", which led to such abominable crimes as the obliteration-bombing of open cities and dropping atom bombs on Japanese cities at a time when Japan was already willing to sign a truce short of unconditional surrender. If anyone doubts that this heritage is still with us, one should read how uncritically influential men can assert that the Second World War was, as far as the U.S.A. is concerned, a "just war".[154]

Is it not also a sign of the pathological condition in which we are living, that even otherwise upright churchmen and politicians easily assert the moral acceptability of the present system of nuclear deterrence, while even the blind can see that the conditions laid out for such acceptability are not a bit better fulfilled now than they were forty years ago?

One churchman called this acceptability, under well-defined conditions, a "last respite". But we may ask: "Is it not cruel to let this sword of Damocles hang over the head of all humankind for half a century without making one real step towards the fulfilment of irrenounceable conditions, and still call this acceptable?"

Only if we are fully aware of the extremely pathological character of our mutual nuclear threat, of the devilish foe-images, of the undigested burden of the past, and of the present boasting of military strength, can we approach with great sensitivity the problems, in a therapeutic spirit and manner. Only thus is there still hope.

A sign of hope is the growing attention given to civilian, nonviolent defence following the spirituality and method of Gandhi's *satyagraha*: a transarmament which, in my eyes, is possible only if we discern the pathological situation with the merciful eyes of the therapist and if we approach transarmament mainly in the perspective of healing public life and at the same time healing ourselves from all contamination through violence.

NOTES

135. *Bischöfe zum Frieden*, Bonn 1983, 180.

136. *Gerchtigkeit schafft Frieden*, Bonn 1983, 18.

138. J. Topel, *The way of peace*, 83.

139. I. Baldermann, *Der Got des Friedens und die Götter der Macht*, 97.

140. The instruction on some aspects of the "theology of liberation" issued by the Congregation for the Faith on August 6, 1984, XI/7, is most explicit against the use of violence: "Violence degrades the dignity in those on whom it is inflicted and equally on those who apply it".

141. Cf. F. Alt, *Friede ist möglich. Die Politik der Bergpredigt*, München 1983; E. Eppler, *Die tödliche Utopie der Sicherheit*, Reinbek 1983.

142. Cf. R. Schwager, *Der Glaube, der die Welt verwandelt*, Mainz 196; Id., *Brauchen wir einen Sündenbock? Gewalt und Erlösung in den Biblischen Schriften*, München 1978; Id., Der geliebte Sohn und die Rotte der Gewalttäter. Christilogie und Erlösungslehre", in: J. Blank und G. Hasenhütl (eds.), *Glaube an Jesus Christus*, Düsseldorf 1980, 117–133.

143. I. Baldermann, *Der Gott des Friedens und die Götter der Macht*, 77.

144. C. F. von Weizsäcker, *Der ungesicherte Friede*, 24.

145. T. Merton, *Faith and Violence*, 80.

146. R. May, *op. cit.*, 186, 166, 53.

147. H. E. Bahr, *Versöhnung und Widerstand*, 69f. Cf. G. Angers, *Die atomare Bedrohung*, München 1981, 94.

148. Cf. H. Vetschera, "Rüstungsentwicklung und Rüstungskontrolle", in E. Lorenz (ed.), *Kirchen und Frieden*, 91–101.

149. Declaration of the General Synod of the Nederlandse Hervormde Kerk, quoted by H. U. Kirchhoff, *Kirche und Kernbewaffnung*, Neukirchen 1981, 109.

150. W. Schmithals, "Die westdeutsche Friedenbewegung in der Einschätzung eines Theologen", in: E. Lorenz (ed.), *Kirchen für den Frieden*, Stuttgart 1983, 130.

151. Lenin, *Gesammelte Werke*, vol. 23, 92, here quoted according to M. Voslensky, "Der Friedensgedanke in der politischen Philosophie und Ethik des Sowjetsaates", in: E. Lorenz (ed.), *Kirchen für den Frieden*, 83–89.

152. Lenin, *Werke*, vol. 23, 72.

153. Lenin's letter to Titscherin of February 16, 1922, in: Lenin, *Friefe*, vol. 9, 175; cf. 481.

154. Cf. W. V. O'Brien, "Just War Doctrine in a Nuclear Context", in: *Theological Studies* 44 (1983), 191–221. The author not only asserts that the use of nuclear weapons can be eventually justified on the basis of the just war theory, but also that there is a worldwide conviction that on the part of the allies the Second World War was a model of a "just war".

CHAPTER SIX

Away from self-destructive deterrence, towards a healing civilian defence

1. *And yet, there is hope*

The peace-ethics of the Church has reached a new phase since the popes called constantly for liberation from the slavery of war and for nonviolent solutions. This is especially evident after several influential Bishops' Conferences, eminent Church leaders like Cardinal Martini of Milan[155] and, above all, the U.S. Bishops, after long years of deliberation and with convincing competence and hard work, have called almost unanimously for serious consideration of the alternative of civilian defence. Of "nonviolent popular defence" they say: "Once we recognize that the almost certain consequences of existing politics and strategies of war carry with them a very real threat to the future existence of humankind itself, practical reason as well as spiritual faith demands that it be given serious consideration as an alternative course of action".[156]

For the project of nonviolent popular defence, partial actualizations and first steps are already a therapeutic approach and challenge for all nations. Rightly understood, it calls for a broader therapeutic approach to many evils of our sick culture and society. This can be seen as the therapeutic introduction of a creative crisis which, in view of the enormously pathological situation, should not be underrated. Yet, if everything is done with healing understanding and love, the crisis, of itself, might turn out to be history's most relevant leap in human advancement. The very sacrifices required in the necessary preparation and transition can help the other camps to realize that their own future may gain the most if they are willing to respond to the signals of peace through transarmament.

The very substance of this transarmament is that the goal is nothing less than to heal humankind from inclinations to and ideologies of violence. It points to the new weapons of peace described by the Letter to the Ephesians and applied in historical adaptations by Gandhi and Martin Luther King. These new weapons and attitudes are just the opposite of those of warrior tribes of the past, when bloody "triumphs" and "honours" were sought by bellicose soldiers and politicians.

All weapons for killing, from the most ancient to today's nuclear warheads, are signs of contempt for human life. The transarmament of which we speak is the very fruit of respect and love for all life, for all people. Its motivation is on a totally different level from the armament race, and shows the humane quality of a renewed faith in the meaning and purpose of human history. The "sacrifices" required by such transarmament contradict the bloody sacrifices of war; they draw their force from the renconciling sacrifice of the Redeemer of the world.[157]

It is my deep conviction that, in this historical situation, God wants us to render this concrete service to the gospel of peace and nonviolence. I think we have far better reasons to cry out "God wills it!" than St Bernard of Clairvaux had when he preached the crusade to be carried out with the weaponry of the old, unredeemed world.

The transarmament of which we speak is not totally new. The situation is new, and the breadth of the approach. One of the first to propose new models of defence under the name of "social defence" — or civilian or popular nonviolent defence as inspired by Gandhi — was the Norwegian peace researcher, Johan Galtung. He profited also from some valuable experiences made by the Danish and Norwegian resistance during Hitler's regime.

Gandhi, by wholly moral means, succeeded in forcing the greatest world-power of that time, the well-established colonialist, England, to restore independence to India. The greatest psychological effect was that India, as a befriended nation, decided to be a part of the British Commonwealth. It was not a "defeat" of the British army and its Indian mercenaries, but rather a wholesome awakening of the British people. This shows that popular (civilian) nonviolent defence can build bridges to world populations, bridges even to former colonialist powers.

It is the hope of peace researchers,[158] who advocate and explore civilian nonviolent defence, that a nation adopting the nonviolent model can give strong and sympathetic signals of hope and challenge to neighbouring nations and their governments.

As a first step, war-minded superpowers might only be able to understand this model as a different mode of "deterrence" whereby (1) in the case of taking advantage and trying to submit the "disarmed" nation, they have to fear that their own population, including many soldiers, will refuse to participate or co-operate in an invasion; (2) in any case, they would draw no advantage from an act of invasion and occupation, since civilian resistance by non-co-operation would frustrate all their purposes; (3) their ideologies and political ambitions would be unmasked in the face of the whole world; they would at once appear as abominable criminals to the conscience of all reasonable people and their own citizens. All this, however, is only a matter of a first phase. The full hope of a nation transarmed to absolute peaceful, nonviolent means is much more ambitious. It is to win over the people and governments of the other side — the opponents — for the same approach to life and politics: to free all from the hell of violent deterrence.

2. *More than an urgent surgery: a unique chance*

Transarmament, at this crossroad of human history, is a matter of extreme urgency. But once we have fully understood its healing power, its unique implications and hoped-for results, it will mean much more to us. After hominization, millions of years ago, it would be the greatest qualitative leap towards a more authentic humanness. We see in it a "*kairos*", a great chance. And that is the way it should be proposed to public conscience.

Pope John Paul II describes the situation: "Thus the nuclear terror which attacks our era moves humanity to enrich its common heritage by a very simple discovery, easily accessible: that war is the most barbarous and most ineffective means to solve conflicts".[159] This discovery, expressed in a first-moment negative context, becomes an eye-opening "*kairos*" when we recognize the real alternative: a radical conversion of tremendous breadth, a most creative, solidary task of putting to work all the promptings from the gospel of peace and nonviolence, and taking up the armour of peace for the ordering of social, cultural and political life.

The Second Vatican Council, when it spoke of the prospect of humankind freeing itself from the slavery of war under the pressure of the untenable situation in our era, drew attention to the positive offer of God, quoting the peace-message of the Gospel: "The hour of my favour has now come; now, I say, has the day of deliverance dawned" (2 Cor 6:2).[160] In our greatest need, God can offer us a unique sign of hope and salvation.

F. X. Meehan speaks of an "exciting kairotic moment", and gives the following reason: "We are literally pulled by historic circumstances to rediscover the early Christian witness and transformation from within". But Meehan thinks not only of a principle for individual lifestyle but of "nonviolence as a decisive principle of life and politics".[161] And already in 1950, George Orwell, reminding us of Gandhi's warning that only nonviolence could save Europe, expressed his reflection that a radical conversion to nonviolence might well be the only exit from the present situation.[162]

Not only professional peace researchers like Ulrich Albrecht, Theodor Ebert, John Galtung, Arne Naess, Gene Sharp and Carl F. von Weizsäcker, but countless other humane people have come to the conclusion that a profound conversion to nonviolence, with its systematic and competent application through civilian defence, is the only viable, morally good solution in extreme need; but much more, they see it as an epochal opportunity. Even highly ranked military professionals have come to the same conclusion, starting from the proven disproportionality of today's means of warfare for restoring peace.[163]

Only through faith, or at least through insight into the healing power of nonviolence as principle of life and politics, can the present catastrophic danger be transformed into a positive opportunity. This does not say that we simply stand before a lucky chance. There are risks inherent, as we shall see. Yet these risks are small in comparison with the terror of "deterrence" and its consequences.

Those who are willing to carry out the project of nonviolent citizen defence might risk even their lives, but their risks and sacrifices are not self-defeating, whereas killing others is. If the advocates of social defence believe in the fundamental goodness of all peoples, they will want to speak to the hearts of the people of an invading or oppressing force, to lay before them the nobility of peace and nonviolence. Soldiers, touched by heart-to-heart dialogue, will yield less easily to orders from oppressive leaders for any brutal procedures. As in the case of Gandhi's "salt-*satyagraha*" campaign, mercenaries, driven by threats and instigated by promises, might sometimes act with extreme cruelty against disarmed, peace-loving people; but, generally, the risk of life will be the less if the nonviolent acts are carried out with the stubborn courage of conviction.

To the extent that charismatic men and women dedicate themselves to this noble task with competence, good argument, and great love for all those involved, including the opponents: to that extent today's need can be transformed into the most providential chance of our epoch. The dedication brought to this cause must be at least no less than the intelligence, courage, money and risks offered to the cruel cause of war. Anyone who understands what is at stake will face confidently the proportionate loss or gain. Beyond the question of "success", the very decision for nonviolent defence by people, whole communities and nations, would be the most wonderful gain, "a spiritual upheaval such as seldom recorded in history. But such things have happened, and let us hope we have not gone so far that they will not happen again".[164] However, the question is whether people who are so ensnared in the present pathological situation will be able to grasp the great chance.

3. *Comparative risk assessment*

One of the most important sentences in the U.S. Bishops' pastoral letter, "The Challenge of Peace", might well be history-shaping or at least contributing essentially to a turn in Catholic theology and public opinion: "Nonviolent means of resistance to evil deserve much more study than they thus far received". In the following pages I give my response to the Bishops' warning, "Before the possibility is dismissed as impractical and unrealistic, we urge that it be measured against the almost certain effects of a major war".[165]

In such a comparative assessment we have to avoid a naked utilitarianism which would look only to such "values" as "success", material losses and gains, economic freedom of competition and chance to grow richer still. As in all authentic teleological efforts, prime attention must be given to the foreseeable consequences of a choice or an option at the level of the morally relevant foreseeable results.

I hope to find a good number of English-writing theologians and peace researchers ready for a new thinking on the basis of a teleological comparative gain-and-risk assessment of the only two real options: to accept a policy of some kind of military deterrence or to make a firm solidary commitment to a spirituality and strategy of nonviolent defence of basic human values and rights.

Let us be realistic and see that the option has to be made in the present historical context, in which two antagonistic superpowers have at their disposal not only an incredible nuclear-overkill arsenal, but also tremendous quantities of other kinds of still more cruel weapons.[166]

First, let us see the benefits and risks of simply dismissing the nonviolent alternative as unrealistic.

For highly relevant moral values, the foreseeable certain negative and high risks are innumerable. Forty years of complete failure to halt the arms race, the development of ever new nuclear and chemical weaponry, and the arms trade leave us only grim hopes that this will soon change without the alternative option for nonviolent defence. And what about the morally relevant hope that the system of deterrence, which gave the U.S.A. and its West European allies four decades of peace, will continue to "guarantee" this kind of peace? With the most outstanding and impartial peace researchers, I think this hope is extremely shaky.

My reasons to doubt such a "guarantee" are well grounded. Under the umbrella of nuclear deterrence, both the U.S.A. and Russia have been fighting wars in which millions of people have been killed, mutilated or benumbed. And repeatedly, in the course of these wars and some other conflict-situations, an escalation into nuclear war was seriously considered. Both military blocks have filled not only their own but also the whole world's arsenals with their sophisticated "traditional" weapons, creating in many parts of the world ever more explosive situations which, one day, might involve the superpowers in direct confrontation. Further, given the mechanism of the military-industrial complex, the deadly weight of economic and political hegemonism and the unavoidably worsening foe-images, the risks of escalation are constantly increasing.

It is not very realistic to philosophize on a "still acceptable" tolerance of nuclear deterrence, with our neatly defined conditions for such tolerance, while leaving out of our assessment the fact that, up to now, none of these conditions is fulfilled. And given the widespread mentality on both sides of the military blocks, we have to fear the worst of immoral actions. An influential man in Washington, a Georgetown University government professor, stated that "Unlimited nuclear war could be justified as the most desperate measure" (note the word "justified"). "A decision to engage in such a war would be made not so much in virtue of the military necessities of 'winning' the object of the conflict, but rather in virtue of the desire to deny the victor the fruits of his victory".[167]

Here we are faced not with just a false teleological assessment, but with a shocking immorality of thought and communication, and of the grave complicity — or pseudo-innocence — of people who passively let such communication go out to our citizens when we know very well how it will impress the other side of the military block.

Add to all this the evident insight expressed by Rollo May: "No one can have the slightest doubt that war does erode individual responsibility and the autonomy of conscience". Concretely, for all too many people this means to "give one's conscience over to the group",[168] the "group" being the decision makers who think just as the communicator does!

The extremely high risk of a final escalation into military confrontation, and finally into nuclear escalation, will be worsened when Christian ethicists dare to justify, on principle, some limited use of nuclear weapons, without realistically assessing not only the immediate cost in human lives but also the enormous risk of full scale escalation as soon as the nuclear threshold is once transgressed.

But the assessment of the foreseeable, real risks does not allow us to forget for one moment the non-values of the present system of nuclear deterrence, with little or no hope for any essential improvement as long as the alternative of nonviolent defence of human values, like freedom, is not even taken into account. Meanwhile, the arms race and big business go on, poisoning the world and the whole economic exchange. This whole game needs the fabric of devilish foe-images. The military-industrial complex will grow stronger and "guarantee" that things are getting worse.

If a considerable effort is not made, even by Christians and believers in one God, Father of all, to win over public conscience for the nonviolent alternative and a thorough cultural, educational and socio-economic change as part of that option, there is scarcely any chance to solve the North-South conflict. And the chance to bring forth a radical change for social justice at all levels, especially on the planetarian level, will be sorely lessened.

As people become more and more used to co-operating — in pseudo-innocence — for a system of mutual threat and collective egotism, there will be less and less chance of conversion to a world-wide solidarity, of co-operation in fighting worldwide misery and starvation, of solving serious ecological crises and preventing an ecological disaster.

As long as the talents and time of the most gifted people are used for the military-industrial complex and its built-in system of arms race, arms sales and deterrence, the general moral level of citizens, the educational system and public opinion will steadily deteriorate. Terrorism and general criminality does and will increase with the gross national product, and even more when the average people see the appalling standards by which the powerful justify themselves and their present system of power.

The pro-life movement is weakened to the extent that any of its members, while fighting against abortion and similar evils, will not free themselves radically from complicity with the system of deterrence and all the evils it implies, and from all forms of pseudo-innocence which develop under the umbrella of "deterrence".

People who accept the given system for the defence of their "freedom" will not realize how bloated their concern is for economic-competitive freedom and freedom for consumerism, to the detriment of psychological and spiritual freedom. Without repentance and conversion in the broadest sense, we will not free ourselves "from the burden of the past".[169] To my mind, the minimum condition and requirement for such an encompassing new thinking is not possible to those who do not even give serious consideration to the nonviolent alternative.

I agree wholeheartedly with Richard McSorley's statement that "until we squarely face the question of our consent to use nuclear weapons, any hope of large scale improvement in public morality is doomed to failure".[170] Personally, I cannot realistically conceive of a radical dissociation from consent to use nuclear weapons, without commitment to the nonviolent alternative and a serious effort to win over a democratic majority for it.

Last but not least, one of the greatest risks of the present system of coupled deterrence by the socio-economic superpowers is the perpetuation of the bureaucratic system of Communism: the hawks in the Kremlin needing the hawks in the Pentagon to keep themselves in power. Vast populations are forced into an almost fatalistic acceptance of the Communist protection against the nuclear threat from the West. The undeniable fermentation within the populations governed by totalitarian Communist regimes is blocked to a great extent by our system of deterrence and all the frightening things implied by it. If, on our side, one of the main reasons for continuing global terror is to "keep our privileged place in the world", then how can we contradict Bishop Hunthausen, who firmly asserts that "any nation, which makes as its first priority the building up of armaments and not the creative work of peace and disarmament, is immoral"?[171]

At this crossroad of human history, a failure to give very serious consideration to the nonviolent alternative undermines the credibility of our faith in the Redeemer of the *world* (not only of "souls"!). My way of adhering to faith in the Redeemer of the world and redemption does not allow me to say: "If the Christian community is to be faithful to the full meaning of the Paschal Mystery as the inauguration of the kingdom of God, there must be a pluralism of ethical stances within it. I would conclude, therefore, that both the pacifist ethic and the just war ethic are legitimate and necessary expressions of Christian faith".[172] Yet, one must see that this statement by David Hollenbach is a gigantic step forward in comparison with the writings of moralists of one or two decades ago, especially since the "just war" theory is so well presented by the author.

I understand that we have to accept respectfully the given pluralism, but, as I see it, we have to work firmly at this critical time to rid ourselves of the "just war" theory, especially while it remains so distorted in the minds and writings of many Catholics. For the time being, the U.S. Bishops could do no more than to appeal to all to give serious consideration to the nonviolent alternative. If this is done, a healing process is already set in motion. The goal cannot be a perpetuated pluralism but a solidary option for nonviolent defence.

Let us now see the risks taken by taking the option for an exclusively nonviolent defence of basic human rights.

The first and perhaps the greatest risk is to pour new wine into old skins by simply looking for new strategies without the underlying spirituality. Using Skinnerian conditioning in order to make people — one's own people or the other side's — powerless and docile, is pouring corrupt and new wine into bad old skins. Whoever reads attentively Rollo May's book *Power and Innocence* will see how dangerous the Skinnerian behaviour modification would be as a way to overcome violence. The kind of powerlessness that such methods and tactics produce is the very "breeding ground" for violent explosions. The reason nonviolence worked in the cases of Gandhi and Martin Luther King is because it was an authentic expression of profound spirituality. A nonviolent option would fall short if it lacked an awareness of the need for ongoing conversion and watchfulness over the dragon or sphinx in oneself.

Nonviolence has little chance if it is proposed only as second choice when a nation is already militarily defeated. It just cannot work in people who, by warlike attitudes and through devastating fighting — and imbued with age-old foe-images — have been demoralized.

Risks are still very high if the option is fundamentally sincere but underpinned by the hope that it is a cheaper solution than the costs of military deterrence. It surely does not risk life as much as the present approach to military defence; but it requires greater inner strength and a readiness to aim for higher moral standards. And even an imperfect start in the right direction towards a nonviolent culture can open new horizons and, in time, bring new breakthroughs.

4. *Fully recognizing the pathological point of departure*

We have come to realize that, facing the nuclear threat, blame, anguish and guilt feelings will not save us. The Redeemer did not come to judge and condemn but to heal the sick. This must be the norm of our approach. There is great need for healing compassion, and all the more because we all are somehow entangled in the pathological situation. Only in the progress of healing can people realize how much stupidity and guilt have been involved.

Surely there is need of appeal to people's conscience, need of a moral and religious conversion; but everything must be done in a sober therapeutic approach. One cannot confront a gravely sick person just as a moralist. Only in the process of recovery might the proper moment come to face directly the question of responsibility, accountability and restitution. The healer must sympathize with the difficulties of the other in the course of conversion to a new thinking and a firm fundamental option for nonviolence.

I feel that peace research and peace pedagogy must give much closer attention to the therapeutic dimension which, up to now, has been generally neglected. There is also need to study social therapy as a discipline. Peace researcher, Dieter Senghaas, writes that a peace policy oriented to "a politics of deterrence which hangs on a very thin thread of ethical justification" is counter-productive because of its pathological context.[173] However, it does not follow that we should condemn morally those political leaders who, on this road, are earnestly trying to assure peace. They and we stand before a knot which is pathologically loaded and cannot simply be dissolved or cut through. The only path is through a complicated healing process. Without full attention to the pathology there is little hope for finding an effective therapy. There is even the great danger of forgetting completely that the most needed element is therapy.

The pastoral letter of the West German Bishops speaks of the "monstrosity" of expecting to secure peace by "threatening mass destruction, which can never be allowed".[174] "Monstrosity" is just a strong expression for pathology. Whatever the Bishops say in their pastoral letter makes sense only in a perspective of a thoroughgoing healing process.

Once we have tried to understand the pathology of a whole history of treachery and violence, which constantly seeks self-justification, we must turn our attention even more to our healthy and healing energies.

The first is the strength of faith in the Redeemer and redemption, including especially redemption from violence and lie. In the light of faith we try to discover all the good in ourselves and in our fellowmen, especially in those who oppose us. Then follows the important step of winning over the social elites, especially those most influential in forming public opinion, to commit themselves to the cause of nonviolence and nonviolent defence. Next, we need basic communities of people who learn more about nonviolence and train themselves for this cause. All must constantly help each other to mobilize, in ourselves and others, all the healthy energies and, if needed, to cleanse them and channel them in the right direction. In this field we all should be discoverers and innovators. The redeemed should credit themselves with much more ability than they usually do.

In the same line, the need to be critical of our culture should not seduce us away from its positive aspects. This is of special importance for the project of civilian defence. We must know the values that deserve to be protected and, if need be, defended. Think, for instance, of our democratic liberty, liberty of conscience and religion, space for creative initiatives, and such. It is, then, an essential part of our commitment to preserve and improve all these values, especially the experience of solidarity, subsidiarity, social justice, coresponsibility, and rightful sharing in decision-making processes.

The more our society fulfills the essential requirements of a participatory society, the better we can win people over for civilian defence and for the necessary competence to carry it out. In this context we call attention again to pathological foe-images. Two points require special care. There is a strong feedback whereby a sick foreign politics, operating with foe-images and threats, disturbs also interior politics. Where people are trained to see only enemies in neighbouring peoples, they will react all too easily to fellow-citizens of other groups as if they were enemies.

Added to this is the special problem of the party leaders of the Eastern block. The "hawks" in the Kremlin need the "hawks" in the Pentagon to strengthen their belligerent position and military display. The counterpart in the West is not absent: it is perhaps far more present than we suspect. The military-industrial complex, in its own way, needs the hawks in Moscow. And are not the politicians in the West sometimes more likely to win elections if they promise a politics of power, reacting against the hawks in the East? Things change only if people find out what the real game is. Then social therapy can be more easily applied.

The fact that in the strongest superpower 400,000 (and probably more) highly-gifted scientists use their talents and time entirely for military research and production is, in itself, a pathological symptom. It is also a dangerous virus affecting the whole educational system and weakening the whole social and cultural sectors.[175]

The expenditure for armament in 1984 amounted to about one thousand billion dollars.[176] It has been calculated that 5 per cent of this would be sufficient to fight world hunger effectively and to save hundreds of thousands whose lives and/or health is endangered by insufficient nourishment or lack of medical care. Further, a relatively small portion of this money would suffice to solve the direct ecological problems, such as reforesting the Sahara desert.

One of the dangerous pathologies is the profound ambiguity of the system of deterrence. On the one hand it is said to serve only security and peace, thus preventing the danger of war. On the other hand we hear about training and war games on how to win wars with nuclear weapons. Add to this the ingenuity of political messengers who declare that our political leaders will never use nuclear weapons ("they have them only to prevent war"), while the politicians tell us that they really will display their full power if the enemy does not behave. Note also that two factors meet each other: the danger inherent in the system of deterrence, as such, and the pathological thinking and talking that does not at all sound like peacefulness.[177]

Peace researchers, who study and advocate nonviolent civilian defence, are generally — and with good reason — against a mix of armed defence and nonviolent defence. However, if we could once get public assent and political option for popular defence as the goal to be reached, we could discuss the steps of transition. An intermediate step would be an exclusively defensive army and armament and the effort to persuade the other side to offer the same, in view of our option for a next step, which would be exclusively nonviolent defence. Beyond the general principles, we also have to look for a realistic strategy of transition. One thing must always be clear: everything must be done to get ourselves and all the world out of the trap of deterrence as quickly as possible.

In many respects the procedure for the production and argumentation of the pastoral letter, "The Challenge of Peace", is a good model for an imitatory therapeutic process. Some of the bishops confessed that they themselves gradually experienced a kind of healing and conversion, due to patient dialogue, listening to experts, and so on.

The transarmament for civilian defence is most urgent. No time should be lost. But on the other hand we have to learn that the healing of deeply rooted pathological conditions, both individual and social, needs patience. Impatience, as we noted earlier, is one of the symptoms and causes of violence.

5. *Therapeutic diagnosis and facing creative crises*

The therapeutic approach advocated here needs interdisciplinary co-operation for peace research and peace education. But the whole research and practice needs a new thinking based on our faith in the Redemption.

The model of civilian defence should be understood as "increased normality under abnormal conditions".[178] It implies fostering the healthy functioning of all social structures, processes and services, but in a way that a would-be aggressor or colonialist can realize that nothing will function in his favour. All those involved in any effort of oppression should see that the champions of nonviolent defence have no anguish complexes, no unhealthy fears, no cowardice.

The healthy attitudes of the oppressed must provoke in aggressors and their collaborators a shocking insight to their own pathological condition and action. Indeed, for somehow normal people it must be a shocking — and hopefully therapeutic — experience to meet healthy people who oppose their peacelessness with shining peacefulness. But it is important that the intention of all champions of civilian defence be explicitly the therapeutic effect. Otherwise, hard hearts could harden even more. The enemy is not to be treated as enemy, but as person who will profit if he accepts an advance of trust that he can and will discover in himself the inner goodness that cries for peace. The necessary fearlessness must never appear as contempt for the aggressor.

Promoters of civilian defence have to be prepared to evidence their own nonviolence and their therapeutic charism by the way they react-respond to pathological resistance within their own nation while working to win a consensus, or at least a democratic majority, and after the government's decision in its favour. Those who still oppose it — perhaps even by violent means — are not to be seen as enemies but as people to be reached and healed in their conscience. The creative crisis into which Gandhi brought the British people is well described by Rollo May: "The whole British empire creaked and groaned as it moved to find new ways of dealing with the little brown man who knew how to turn his suffering to constructive use".[179]

It is important to understand the various kinds of crisis that can occur during the process of healing and transition. We must be prepared to meet serious opposition among privileged classes and in parts of the armed forces, whose members have to pass through a kind of identity crisis. The fears and worries of these people have to be understood and patiently dealt with. These people can be helped to understand that their own welfare and wholeness is as much at stake as that of other parts of the population. They should feel that, despite their reluctance, they are expected finally to become valuable promoters of this common cause. Their reactions and arguments have to be taken seriously and treated in a way analogous to the therapist's way of dealing with a crisis of growth.

In view of people's insertion in one of the two power-blocks, more or less pathological reactions may be expected within one's own block. The worst kind of such reaction was experienced in the invasion of Prague by the powers of the Warsaw block. Those who advocate nonviolent popular defence must be prepared psychologically and spiritually and be competent in social and individual therapy, alive to addressing properly both violent opponents and public opinion. They will always play with open cards.

Peace researchers give full attention to a foreseeable effect of destabilization within the Warsaw Pact. Therefore, everything should be avoided that could look like a dishonest imitation of the old power principle, "*Divide et impera*" — Create discord to be the victor. It must be made evident that social defence is not directed against any particular military block, but aims at overcoming the division of the world into power-blocks. The project of popular nonviolent defence is not directed against anyone. Its whole intention is to render a direly needed service to the whole human race.

Undeniable risks are inherent in the difficult transarmament, the transition from the old strategy to nonviolent defence. The risks may come from the military-industrial complex, from would-be dictators of one's own country or of a superpower of the same military block, especially if a well-prepared *putsch* takes place before people have had the necessary training and won the spiritual strength for nonviolent resistance. This kind of risk can become greater if people think only in terms of resisting Communist invaders.

The risk generally feared is that an alien authoritarian power (say, an authoritarian Communist superpower) might take advantage of "disarmament" for aggressive action before the real transarmament for nonviolent culture, strategy and tactic has been sufficiently prepared. So the real fear is that nonviolent defence may not work because too many selfish people and groups might be willing to co-operate with an oppressive invader. In other words, we fear that, under the past and present capitalistic system, we may have lost so much spiritual strength that we cannot recover.

The risk that nonviolent defence might not work is highest in nations where unfair competition and exploitation on both the national and international level is deeply rooted.

Some concentrate only on the danger of "losing our freedom", without asking themselves whether the kind of freedom they mean is economic, psychological or spiritual. Losing our "freedom" to get more wealth, more comfort, more consumption, could be a blessed loss if we discover the unique historical chance to increase our psychological and spiritual strength and freedom by a wholehearted option and consistent application of nonviolent defence of all the basic values inherent in a nonviolent culture.

6. *Central importance of healing communications*

The virtuous art of truthful, peaceful and peace-making communication cannot be overrated. It is one of the pillars of nonviolent defence, of transarmament for peace. The Czechoslovakian population improvised splendidly in this field, as in the whole nonviolent approach. And Johan Galtung thinks that "what they have achieved is only 1 per cent of what they would have been able to achieve after a thoroughgoing preparation".[180]

a) Training in small groups

Gandhi realized very early that basic communities are of paramount importance for acquiring the necessary spirituality, skill and discipline for friendship and cohesion. These basic communities were then the "cadre troops" for all the *satyagraha* actions. In the case of an invasion or a military *putsch*, they must be distributed over the whole territory to animate and co-ordinate the whole population. They have to be well provided and well trained in the use of the most modern means of communication. Part of the training occurs by sharing in all the various efforts in favour of the civilian defence project and in all the initiatives for strengthening the social and cultural values which make social defence worthwhile.

b) Nonviolent communication between the social groupings

Nonviolent communication within the population prepares for emergencies and is, by itself, a great task of nonviolence and genuine healing. It works for a peaceful nation, for solidarity, shared ideals and co-operation. It is a matter of ongoing reconciliation between social classes, political parties and the various cultural groupings.

A special taks is a peaceful and respectful dialogue between conscientious objectors to military service and those whose consciences are enabled or urged to fulfill faithfully their military service. Among those who serve we can surely find people who, by their whole character, might be well qualified for social defence and might gladly choose it if this were to become the official approach. Altogether, it is very important that all men and women in military service receive clear and helpful information about the scope and spirituality of civilian nonviolent defence. They will play a vital role in the time of transition and in cases of emergency. Many who are well trained in communication could be among the cadres of civilian defence.

c) Worldwide communication about the scope of social defence

The project of civilian defence has a future only to the extent that nonviolent and competent information about its meaning, purpose and spirituality, and its healing power for the whole of individual and public life, is spread worldwide. This dialogue must not be looked within the traditional diplomatic channels but should not exclude them. Of course, there must be a competent dialogue with all the governments involved on one side or the other; but it must also become a dialogue among all peoples all over the world. All the usual channels have to be used and new ones have to be discovered. Through such communication mutual fears can be overcome. It can contribute substantially to making all people one worldwide family.

Care must be taken that all means of communication with the outside world are available for emergency cases, and new means must constantly be sought. This is a part of the "new weapons for peace".

Peace researcher E. O. Czempiel illustrates communication by the relationship between the Federal German Republic and East Germany, which is occupied by the Russian army. There has been for a long time no chance whatsoever to solve the question and probably there will never be any, in the way of past nation-states. The appropriate model is a communicative covenant united by bonds of tradition, culture and shared interest in world peace, which works towards overcoming the antagonisms between the military blocks.[181]

d) Signalling firmness of purpose and hopes

Transarmament's purpose to avoid the sad case of emergency is far more convincing than the present system of deterrence. Therefore, all the would-be invaders or *putschists* must be fully and timely informed about what civilian defence means and what they should expect when they meet the absolute firmness and skill of the champions of nonviolence, indeed of the whole population.

This process of information should not appear as threat or as utilitarian cost-and-gain calculation, although a potential aggressor should be made fully aware of the heavy risks of those who would assault a population well prepared for nonviolent defence. The aggressor would then think about the shock to his men when they experience the defence manifestations of a healthy, peaceful nation, the shock of world opinion, the evident risk of discrediting their ideology and bellicose character. If it were done by a Communist "hierarchy", defenders of Marxist orthodoxy, this would probably be the death blow to Marxism forever.

But in the matter of communication, the gentle appeal to join hands in peacefulness and to rejoice in the chance to get out of the deadly trap of deterrence must always stand in the foreground. It should be nothing less than a gracious invitation to celebrate the shared victory over war with no "victor's justice".

NOTES

155. Cardinal Martini, "Sono per la difesa civile nonviolenta", in: *Jesus*, March 1984, 70.

156. "The Challenge of Peace", *Origins*, May 19, 1983, 22.

157. Cf. J. W. Douglas, *The Non-Violent Cross*, 70.

158. Out of an abundant literature I can mention only few works: G. Sharp, *The Politics of Nonviolent Action*, 3 vols., Boston 1974 (a serious flaw in Sharp's earlier publications is a noticeable affinity to some aspects of B. F. Skinner's behaviourism); T. Norbert, *Soziale Verteidigung*, Waldkirch 1982 and 1983. There are specalized periodicals on nonviolent action, in every major language.

159. John Paul II, *Message for the World Day of Peace*, 1982.

160. *Gaudium et Spes*, 82.

161. F. X. Meehan, "The Moral Dimensions of Disarmament", in: *New Catholic World* 226 (1982), 68-70.

162. G. Orwell, "Reflections on Gandhi", in: *Shooting an Elephant*, London 1950, 111.

163. Sir St. King-Hall, *Defence in the Nuclear Age*, Nyak 1959; B. H. Liddel-Hart, *Deterrent or Defense*, New York 1960. On the famous French General Jacques de Bollaridère see: J.-M. Muller, *Vous avez dit 'pacifisme'? De la menace nucléaire à la defense civile non-violente*, Paris 1984.

164. T. Merton, *Faith and Violence*, Notre Dame, 3rd ed. 1976, 118.

165. "The Challenge of Peace", *Origins*, May 19, 1983.

166. David Hollenbach, SJ, *Nuclear Ethics*, New York / Ramsey, 1983, 32, dismisses all too easily the nonviolent alternative, although throughout his whole book he shows a profound understanding and appreciation of nonviolent spirituality. He does so on the basis of an assessment of the historical situation. His interpretation of the "just war" theory is appropriate, and he is rightly critical of the present policy of the government. His conclusion, however, is that "the just war theory still holds a privileged place in the Christian community's efforts to make a contribution to the formation of public policy" (p. 38).

167. W. V. O'Brien, "Legitimate Military Necessity in Nuclear War", in: *World Polity*, Vol. II, (Washington, Georgetown University, The Institute of World Polity, 1980), 79. See G. A. Vanderhaar, *op. cit.*, 30ff, other utterances even more extreme, under the heading "Blow Up the World".

168. R. May, *op. cit.*, 175.

169. R. May, *op. cit.*, 168.

170. R. McSorley, SJ, "It's a Sin to Build a Nuclear Weapon", in: *U.S. Catholic*, October 1976, 12f.

171. Quoted from T. A. Shannon, *What are they saying about peace and war?* New York / Ramsey 1983, 93f.

172. D. Hollenbach, *op. cit.*, 31.

173. D. Senghaas, "Überblick und Ausblick auf Abschreckungspolitik", in: F. Böckle/G. Krell, *Politik und Ethik der Abschreckung*, Mainz 1984, 131f.

174. *Gerechtigkeit schafft Frieden*, 54.

175. Cf. K. Lange-Feldhahn/U. Jäger, *op. cit.* 21.

176. Cf. The yearly publication of SIPRI, *Armament Yearbook*, Reinbeck.

177. Cf. Böckle/Krell, *op. cit.*, 193 and 199; B. Sutor, "Chancen politischer-Innovation durch kirchliche Friedenslehre", in: *St. d. Zeit*, 201 (1983), 230.

178. Lange-Feldhahn, *op. cit.*, 77.

179. R. May, *op. cit.*, 112.

180. J. Galtung, in: *Gewaltfreie Aktion* 3/1 (1970), 31f. I would like to express my opinion that the Czechoslovakian people were not totally unprepared, because the promotion of a Humanist socialism was a great school for creativity, solidarity and communication.

181. E. O. Czempiel, *Friedenssicherung*, in: F. Böckle/G. Krell, *op. cit.*

CHAPTER SEVEN

Strategies of transition towards civilian nonviolent defence

1. *Full consciousness of the difficulties of transition*

The strength of our conviction about the necessity and timeliness of the alternative of nonviolent defence allows and obliges us to face realistically the difficulties of a transition. We have to move from the actual, highly pathological defence system to an unambiguous stance and politics of nonviolence, inseparably united with the firm purpose not to surrender our freedom and our basic human rights. A pathological repression of such an awareness would be a disaster for the very project and for all those involved.

The Evangelical office for military pastoral service speaks frankly about these difficulties. The subject has appeared time and again in their discussions. "The project to develop a system of social defence plays an important role in all debates about alternatives to deterrence. However, it is not yet clear how to make the transition from the present way of avoiding war to an alternative system. This seems the decisive question to be cleared".[182] The advocates of civilian defence are quite aware of these problems and study them intensively. "The difficulty is how to translate the rejection of deterrence into a political strategy".[183]

It would be already a tremendous step forward if all the forces flowing together in today's strong peace movement would finally agree on this one alternative of civilian nonviolent defence, knowing it not only by name but as an essential dimension of the healing gospel of peace.

From numerous discussions with people involved in the peace movement I learned that, once people are set afire by the thought of civilian defence, they tend to feel that pressure should be made on governments to renounce military protection at once. Young idealists especially tend to this direction. They frequently overlook the distinction between "strategy of civilian defence" and "strategies for transition to it".[184]

As far as I can see, most peace researchers speak explicitly about the need for gradualism, and I see no other way for those in positions of responsibility.[185] It is our duty to take into account their situation. But, in any case, it is not possible to make the transition overnight.

Living under democratic regimes, we have many opportunities to advocate civilian defence and to try to win public adherence. If we can win over influential men and women for the project, we can congratulate ourselves. But it would be undemocratic and unrealistic to act as a pressure group for immediate adoption of the project as long as it has no majority support — or almost so. To gain this majority is our immediate task. It needs the best of argumentation, great patience and, at the same time, a strong sense of urgency.

We should not for a moment neglect contact with adherents of the nonviolent alternative who live under totalitarian regimes, including Communist countries or, more precisely, nations governed by Communist parties — which usually do not have real democratic majorities. From the very beginning it is most advantageous to be as much as possible in contact with men and women belonging to the Communist elite, in order to win at least some of them to the ideal of transarmament for nonviolent defence. We have to explore all possibilities to build bridges.

If a Communist party were to decide sincerely for nonviolent defence, this would mean the most profound change in real socialism — or at least in Marxist tradition. Is it utopia? A beautiful dream? It belongs to our vision of redemption that nonviolence will look for all thinkable openings, and give an advance of trust, a challenge for many sincere adherents to socialism. In appealing openly to the populations under Communist regimes, we sincerely address also governments and Communist parties in an open play of the cards.

2. *Points of departure towards new dimensions and a new style of politics*

I see one of the promising starting points in the numerous active and creative groups of Pax Christi. They are indispensable champions of the spirituality and promoters of the project of nonviolent defence, as well as competent communicators for public opinion. There are also other basic communities having similar convictions and competence in dialogue. The scope of these groups is not confined to emergency cases. They find their tasks day by day, unmasking violence, oppression, social injustices and lies, wherever these threaten the common good and contradict a culture of constructive nonviolence.

A pressing field for the practice of militant nonviolence is the fight against the mafia and camorra in Italy and wherever similar groups of violent exploiters are found. Efforts must be made to arouse public conscience and to uncover the dangerous activities of these groups. But at the same time there has to be also the untiring effort to convert the adherents, to speak to their sleeping conscience and to rescue those who, against their own free will, are entangled with them.

The growing number of conscientious objectors should be considered an important potential for basic groups to be formed and trained for civilian defence, especially for the effective use of all modern means of communication for eventual emergencies. A decision by a government to recruit them clearly for this purpose would greatly serve future research and practice.

It can be hoped that from the peace movement, especially from those groups inspired by the gospel of peace, there will arise active groups training for civilian defence. A great diversity of structures and initiatives is not to be feared. Rather, the variety of experiences is helpful for the future. We need as much experience as possible.

It is quite possible that army personnel, too, will produce some groups trained particularly in nonviolent defence. Despite our refusal of the mix of violence-in-defence and nonviolent defence, we should not be disturbed by the fact that, initially, the line might not be clearly drawn in all cases. There is place for gradualism as long as we are clear about our goals.

3. *Groping towards a new style of foreign and international politics*

We imagine here the phase in which individual nations make their option for exclusively nonviolent defence.

Once whole populations are dedicated to a nonviolent culture and nonviolent defence, new insights and hopes will arise. Since these nations will have broken away from the vicious circle of violence and counter-violence, they will have gained an archmedian point from which they can challenge the old system of threat in a quite new way. Healed from age-old pathologies, they can have a missionary and therapeutic mission in the world.

The Gandhi-experience can give us some idea of what can happen if a number of nations decide for nonviolent defence, with all its implications for the whole realm of public and private life. The peace movement should now study past and present cultures which come closest to the ideal of nonviolence as the basic approach to life and politics.

People spiritually and strategically trained for nonviolence could be really "block free" nations and mediators in the tensions between East and West, North and South. They would be best equipped for promoting a new world peace order. From them we can surely expect much greater creativity than from those who still live under the impact of the military-industrial complex. They would be able to bring into the international organization new inspiriations for such basic problems as the ecological problem, aggravated as they are by the armament race, and "development aid" which, at the present time, is so ensnared in the arms-export business of powerful nations that it becomes practically a kind of treachery. I think also of the growth and expansion mania of the highly industrialized nations which seem to need the constant expansion to finance growing armament.

It can be hoped that truly block-free and nonviolent nations will have a stronger voice in the effort to obtain an international ban on all ABC arms.

4. *Various models of transition*

One of the main goals of the present peace politics must be to gradually overcome the division of humankind into distrustful blocks threatening each other by their armament build-ups, their vicious foe-images, and so on. New approaches and a long breath are needed.

Peace researcher Theodor Ebert has studied especially the problem of how nations belonging to one of the military defence pacts

(Atlantic Pact, Warsaw Pact) can make the transition without changing camp and without causing a dangerous destabilization. While "researchers in the field of civilian defence have come to the conviction that the transition to this form of defence within the European community and the Atlantic Pact might be a complex and wearisome process",[186] Ebert believes that it is possible, and not detrimental but even to the advantage of Western countries.[187] Accepting member-states who have opted for civilian defence, NATO countries (Atlantic Pact) would be in a better position to give evidence of their present principle of forming an exclusively defensive pact. Psychologically and morally, they would also be in a better position to make their contribution for the liberation from the trap of deterrence. In a word, they would have a better chance to come effectively to a peace-politics.

Within such a new framework, mutual agreements about nonintervention would have quite different weight. A great leap forward would be the mutual agreement between NATO and the Warsaw Pact to give full freedom to their member-states to choose either pure civilian defence or exclusively defensive armament. Then it might be more hopeful to propose even a disarmed zone (a zone prepared solely for civilian defence) between the two blocks. For instance, on one side might be Norway, Denmark, Holland, the Federal German Republic and so on, and on the other side Poland, East Germany and other block members.

In this way, the countries choosing exclusively nonviolent defence could keep their Western or their Eastern (socialist) structure of society and economy. One should be realistic, however. A real transition to the system of merely social nonviolent defence would bring great movement — a new dynamics — into all the socio-economic, cultural and political relationships and processes. It is easy to imagine that the polarization would quietly diminish and finally disappear. Thus a real chance might arise for a system beyond the present Marxist Communism and beyond Western Capitalism.

5. *Dialogue with Marxists and people raised under Marxism*

There are ecclesiastical circles which react allergically if there is talk about dialogue with socialists and Marxists, and even more if someone states frankly that Western Christians can learn something in the process of such a dialogue.

As a young man I read *Das Kapital* and other works of Karl Marx. I really felt no temptation to become a Marxist, but I became much more sensitive to certain important problems, such as the false use of religion for the benefit of the established order — practically, for the benefit of the rich. I could better understand why the Churches in many countries had lost a large part of the working class.

Behind all of Marx's grave errors and false generalizations there are genuine concerns and a prophetic wrath against oppression and exploitation, especially if done with ideological abuse of religion. His socio-economic analyses have proven erroneous in many cases. And if Marx were to return to life today, he would not recognize himself as "Marxist" in the light of official Marxist doctrine.

If we really want peace in this concrete world and in this historical hour, we must be ready for dialogue with all, including Marxists. We must watch without prejudice the development of thought in the various trends of Marxism. Some of them are hopeful efforts to bring fuller weight to the humanistic dimension of Marx's thought and to promote humanism beyond Marx. There are even beginnings among Marxists that think anew about violence. I point, for instance, to an expression of Ernst Bloch which can find agreement among many less — or more — "unorthodox" Marxists: "Through our social conditions we have increased the evil, the aggressive, the oppressive energies, and ideologized them to such a degree that they appear as original and not as what they are: inflicted on man".[188]

Bloch's words deal with a crucial point in the problem of violence: disputes about an instinct of aggression being or not being part of humanness; whether human aggression must, of necessity, became violence against fellowmen. It is encouraging to hear a Marxist say plainly that, in this matter, we have to be alert about ideologies.

But the dialogue I advocate is not only and not primarily with Marxist philosophers (orthodox or non-orthodox in the judgement of party leaders), but a dialogue with people under Communist party regimes or raised under Communism. We need them as partners to overcome enmity and such great evils as the present system of deterrence. These people have a lot to tell us. Many are disappointed to find so little idealism and generosity among Christians, and are shocked by the quite superficial concept of freedom held by many people in the West. They have a sharp eye for the practical materialism so widespread in the so-called Christian countries of the West. We need a carefully conducted and realistic dialogue.

For mutual therapy and for liberation from so many collective pathologies, we need many channels of dialogue with Marxists and people raised under Marxism. We need cultural and political dialogue, since we want to win all for the cause of peace and social justice. But most basic is the contact with people under Communist regime. They will be our partners as soon as we can assure them credibly that they are no longer "hostages" of nuclear threat from Western regimes.

Our transarmament for nonviolence will be the best assurance for them. We need public opinion in favour of civilian defence not only in our democratic countries, but worldwide. The newest development of means of communication can be providential. The question is how and for what we use them.

NOTES

182. *Was können Kirchen für dem Friden tun?* Ed. by Evangelisches Kirchenamt für die Bundeswehr, Gütersloh, 2nd ed. 1981, 94.

183. T. Risse-Kappen, in: F. Böckle/G. Krell (eds.), *op. cit.*, 212.

184. Cf. B. Häring, *Free and Faithful in Christ*, vol. III, St Paul Publications, Slough 1981, 397-427f.

185. Many impatient people dislike any kind of gradualism. They forget the "art of the possible" and insist that "what is right must be implemented right away". I remember that once, before a large audience, a young lady-theologian called me an "abominable gradualist" when I insisted that we must allow ourselves and others to take the first step before the second.

186. T. Ebert, *Soziale Verteidigung*, vol. 2, 2nd ed., 1983, 73.

187. *Op. cit.*, 179 and 187.

188. E. Bloch, "Die Kategorie der guten Möglichkeit", in: *Evangelische Kommentare*, 8 (1975), 409.

CHAPTER EIGHT

The Church's role to witness to the healing power of nonviolence

The Lord has entrusted to the Church a mission to heal and to reveal the healing power of peace and nonviolence, as an integral part of her mission for salvation and wholeness. The wholeness of the Church herself depends to a great extent on her fidelity to the gospel of peace in her own life and ministry to the world. In the fulfilment of her role, action and prayer must always be joined so that she may never forget that peace and the strength to choose nonviolence are undeserved gifts of God given to those who seek in all things the honour of God, Father of all.

To whatever degree her members yield only to social activism, without the religious dimension and without care for the contemplative calling of true adorers of God, the Church is powerless. "As it cries out to its Lord for healing, it not only proclaims but also models the process of salvation".[189] John Topel rightly insists that, in fulfilment of her mission to bring the gospel of peace to all people, the Church needs constant conversion and renewal for the life of the world. "In many ways, the soul of the conversion of the world will take place at the level of individual conversion, and especially at the level of small communities such as the Catholic Worker community, l'Arche, etc. These communities exemplify and proclaim the dynamics of self-giving love in themselves and in their care for others".[190]

The peace mission concerns the whole Church, the people of God and its pastors. What is most needed on all sides is concrete prophetic realization.

1. *Healing and revealing by discovering the deeper dimensions of faith*

In the past years practical engagement for the gospel of peace has grown in intensity among all the Churches. An ecumenical consensus arises in all the important questions. We can see that "the process of discernment in the local Churches and in the Church universal are evidently entering into a new and fruitful relationship".[191] From many directions the U.S. Bishops are being credited with a triple competence in the preparation of their pastoral letter which gained worldwide attention: a well-founded actualization of the theological tradition, a sober distinction between general principles and their application to today's situation, and special competence in interdisciplinary debate. "The quality of the pastoral letter is due, above all, to the fact that the authors have acquired this competence through the years".[192]

A part of the growing convergence is the careful effort to apply the ethos of the Sermon on the Mount to the life of Christians and their political responsibilities. A central task of the pastors of the Church is the integral and credible proclamation of the gospel of peace, including, above all, healing nonviolence in the perspective of the all-embracing redemption. At this juncture in history, to neglect the message and practice of nonviolence could easily make the Church and her teaching seem irrelevant. But the real question is one of faithfulness to Christ, knowing Christ in his nonviolent, long-suffering love, redeeming and healing sinners.

Christians have to learn, as a most substantial part of their faith, that peace with God, peace in their hearts, peace with neighbour, love of enemy, and reconciliation cannot be separated; they are one indivisible gift of God and a mission for all believers. In this perspective, too, the celebration of peace in the Eucharist, in ongoing thanksgiving, is of vital importance.

From the faith which the Church proclaims, celebrates and lives, there arises a deep consciousness of the solidarity of humankind before God. In this regard Pope John XXIII showed himself a great apostle of peace. The day after his election he wrote in his *Journal of a Soul*: "The whole world is my family. This sense of believing must give character and vigour to my mind, my heart and my actions".[193] With John XXIII and Gandhi in view, James Douglas writes: "The degree to which a person will justify violence and war is in inverse proportion to the depth of his awareness of the bonds of the human family".[194]

Gandhi, inspired by the Gospel, speaks of an infallibility of all who truly believe in the *one* God and Father, whereby they know from within that no man may abuse a woman, no group exploit or oppress another group, no nation colonize and enslave another nation. If we Christians adhere to Christ, the Redeemer of humankind and of the world, we realize that we are never allowed to declare any living person a hopeless case. For Christians, redemption clearly implies being set free for nonviolence and healing love of enemies. It is lack of faith if this gospel does not shine through in us.

Are we ready to profess, with Gandhi: "It is an article of faith that no man has fallen so low that he cannot be redeemed by love"? Gandhi also says: "In the long run nonviolence cannot work in those who have not a living faith in the God of love".[195] It is the noblest and most privileged ministry of the Church to live and to foster such a faith in the God of love, revealed in his Son Jesus Christ. Thus orthodoxy and orthopraxis will not be sundered.

Whoever loves with all his heart and proclaims the integral gospel of peace has a good chance to awaken faith and to win people for peace making and nonviolence. I think that in this respect the personal experience of Robert Jungk is not untypical. He openly confesses that he grew up with the prejudice that "religion is the opium of the people", but that contact with Christians who, by the strength of faith, are committed to the gospel of peace and act faithfully in accordance with it, changed his mind. He adds: "Believers are better prepared than their secularist companions to deal with unavoidable unsuccess".[196]

2. *The healing Church in co-operation with all people of good will*

In dialogue with people who do not share her faith, the Church has to be faithful to her identity which she has in the Gospel. She may never or in any way put the gospel of peace "under the tub" (cf. Mt 5:14). She has to give integral witness to it. Gandhi was guided by the Sermon on the Mount. There are many religious people — even Humanists who belong to no religion — who are attracted by the Sermon, including what it has to say on nonviolence. But they ask the Church critically whether she believes wholeheartedly in the Gospel and takes it as norm for her life.

The word of a Jewish theologian is typical: "The peace programme of the Sermon on the Mount is a vision which may never be betrayed. Woe to us if we unlearn active hope!"[197] Although, in its fullness, the message of nonviolence has its roots in the mystery of redemption through Jesus Christ, faith in the one God, Father of all, and historical insights can serve as a good provisional basis for dialogue on this message.

A distinctively Christian faith tells us that the grace of redemption can and does work also beyond the confines of the institutional Church and even among those who have not yet found full faith in Christ. Where the question is not so much about revelation as about concrete solutions for today's problems — solutions which do not flow directly and for all times from the Gospel itself — theologians and the Magisterium have to use convincing ethical and rational arguments. Hence, "concrete proposals of Christianity for peace and disarmament must be of the kind that universal reasonableness finds convincing and indispensable".[198]

It seems that in some areas the Church asserts too much, but in the matter of peace and nonviolence many people think that she could and should be more decisive. Even those outside the Church would probably agree with Richard McCormick: "We believe that the time has come when the Churches must unequivocally declare that the production and deployment, as well as the use of nuclear weapons, are a crime against humanity, and that such activities must be condemned on ethical and theological grounds".[199] Is it not now evident that the superpowers in the nuclear arms race have not at any time observed any of the conditions which Church leaders considered indispensable for finding the present system of deterrence still somehow tolerable? How long can we continue to speak of a "last resort"?

On the other hand, when the question is how the powerful nations can get out of the hellish "deterrence" trap, we have to try to combine prophetical challenge with a kind of realism, and remind ourselves of the "art of the possible" when we urge those in authority to work more credibly for disarmament and against nuclear threat. For the official Church, the troublesome fact is that the only morally acceptable alternative — that of civilian defence — is not yet sufficiently taught and understood, and the Church itself has not yet done its utmost except, perhaps, in these very latest moments. We are grateful to the episcopal conferences which, with the Holy Father, appeal for greater and more urgent attention to this question.

3. *The Church called to be a model of a healing, nonviolent community*

Being called to share in the healing and nonviolent redemption and peace-mission of Christ imposes on all Christians — and particularly on those who have the special vocation to proclaim and promote peace — a heart-searching examination. Christianity as a whole should be a model. "Christians harbouring distrust against each other, Churches living in discord, do no justice to their peace mission".[200]

The more the whole Church dedicates herself to her mission, the more she will feel the challenge from within to be converted to this very gospel, and the more strongly she will feel the motivation to promote the cause of Christian unity. Herein must all the virtues characterizing peacefulness and nonviolence be cultivated. "Only the countenance of a Church configured with the nonviolent, crucified God can begin again to radiate from within".[201]

It will be good when the Church as a whole, and every Christian, understands this mission and this ongoing conversion according to the model of the "wounded healer".[202] This will not only help to increase therapeutic sensitivity, the indispensable mercy, and strengthen the sense of solidarity, but also will make us more attentive to the danger of being contaminated by a violent culture or even of increasing its contagious potential.

I just want to mention one factor in the strength of truth which is part and parcel of nonviolence. We Christians, including theologians — who have a sometimes troublesome prophetic mission — must remind ourselves that the Church and Church authorities have a right to and are in need of our absolute sincerity and frankness, which is not possible without a careful purification of motives. And the Church authorities must learn, time and again, to favour gratefully such sincerity and to avoid everything that would jeopardize mutual trust and sincerity. In order to remove everything that might work as an institutionalized temptation, a sober look has to be given to any procedure that tends to punish sincerity and remunerate lack of frankness and veracity.

4. *The hour of the laity*

The Second Vatican Council spoke eloquently of the responsibility of the laity in healing public life.[203] Everything that has been said on this point applies to peace-mission. Laypeople stand on the front line. Many bear immediate responsibility for peace in their nations and in the world, and many have the knowledge, experience and particular competence that are seldom accessible to members of the clergy and the Hierarchy.

Cardinal Casaroli, in an address given in San Francisco, emphasised the indispensable role of the laity in such works as peace research and peace education. This does not diminish the Magisterium's special role but, rather, strengthens its impact. "It has likewise always been part of their ministry to the sons and daughters of the Church. . . . What will matter is that people are educated to become peacemakers. It is imperative that peace studies be even more developed in all centres of higher learning, in particular in Catholic colleges and universities, and that peace research becomes more and more an integral part of the commitment and contribution that Catholics make in the academic community".[204]

It is an encouraging sign that at the present time committed Christians stand in the forefront of peace research, and particularly of nonviolence and nonviolent defence systems. The pastoral letter of the U.S. Bishops, "The Challenge of Peace", proves how fruitful the co-operation with competent laypeople was and can be.

NOTES

189. J. Topel, *The Way of Peace*, 144.
190. *Op. cit.*, 145.
191. E. J. Nagel, "Ergebnis langer Debatten. Zur Entstehung des Amerikanischen Friedenshirtenbrief", in: *Herderkorrespondenz*, 37 (1983) 312.
192. *L.c.*, 315.
193. John XXIII, *Journal of a Soul*, New York 1965, 299.
194. J. W. Douglas, *op. cit.*, 84.
195. Quoted by P. Régamey, *op. cit.*, 199 and 197.
196. R. Jungk, *Das Menschenbeben. Der Aufstand gegen das Unerträgliche*, München 1983, 89.
197. P. Lapide, *Wie liebt man seine Feinde*, Mainz 1984, 74.

198. A. Boyens, "Ein gemeinsames Wort der Kirchen zum Frieden", in: E. Lorenz (ed.), *Kirchen für den Frieden*, Stuttgart 1983, 59.

199. R. A. McCormick, "Notes on Moral Theology", in: *Theological Studies*, 45 (1984), 129.

200. W. Schmithals, in: E. Lorenz (ed.), *op. cit.*, 132.

201. H. Spaemann, "Die Stunde der Gewaltlosigkeit", *l.c.*, 86.

202. B. Häring, *Healing and Revealing*, St Paul Publications, Slough 1984, 86-97.

203. Text published in: Pontifical Commission "Justice and Peace", special issue *Commitment to Peace*, 6 (1984), 3-19, quote 18.

204. Text published in: Pontifical Commission "Justice and Peace", special issue *Commitment to Peace*, 6 (1984), 3-19, quote 18.